Christian Character Qualities
Family Nights Tool Chest

Creating Lasting Impressions for the Next Generation!

Jim Weidmann and Kurt Bruner
with Mike and Amy Nappa

Cook Communications

Heritage Builders

This book is dedicated to the men who helped start the Family Night movement: Bob Strauch, Bruce Lester, Del Van Essen, Kirk Weaver, Ron Wilson, and John Warner. May God bless your families and your leadership efforts.

Victor Books is an imprint of
Cook Communications, Colorado Springs, Colorado 80918
Cook Communications, Paris, Ontario
Kingsway Communications, Eastbourne, England.

HERITAGE BUILDERS/FAMILY NIGHT TOOL CHEST, BOOK 3
© 1998 by Jim Weidmann and Kurt Bruner

First edition 1998

Edited by Eric Stanford
Design by Bill Gray
Cover and Interior Illustrations by Guy Wolek

ISBN 0-78143-014-3

Printed and bound in the United States of America
05 04 03 02 01   10 9 8 7

Heritage Builders/Family Night Tool Chest, Book 3, is a Heritage Builders book, created in association with the authors at Nappaland Communications. To contact Heritage Builders Association, send e-mail to: Hbuilders@aol.com.

Contents

Family Nights About Christian Character Qualities

The Heritage Builders Series

This resource was created as an outreach of the Heritage Builders Association—a network of families and churches committed to passing a strong heritage to the next generation. Designed to motivate and assist families as they become intentional about the heritage passing process, this series draws upon the collective wisdom of parents, grandparents, church leaders, and family life experts, in an effort to provide balanced, biblical parenting advice along with effective, practical tools for family living. For more information on the goals and work of the Heritage Builders Association, please see page 114.

Kurt Bruner, M.A.
Executive Editor
Heritage Builders Series

@ Introduction

There is toothpaste all over the
plastic-covered table. Four young
kids are having the time of their lives
squeezing the paste out of the tube—trying
to expunge every drop like Dad told them
to. "Okay," says Dad, slapping a twenty-
dollar bill onto the table. "The first person to
get the toothpaste back into their tube gets
this money!" Little hands begin working to
shove the peppermint pile back into rolled-
up tubes—with very limited success.

Jim is in the midst of a weekly routine in the
Weidmann home when he and his wife spend time creating "impression points" with the kids. "We can't do it, Dad!" protests the
youngest child.

"The Bible tells us that's just like your tongue. Once the words
come out, it's impossible to get them back in. You need to be careful
what you say because you may wish you could take it back." An
unforgettable impression is made.

Impression points occur every day of our lives. Intentionally or
not, we impress upon our children our values, preferences, beliefs,
quirks, and concerns. It happens both through our talk and through
our walk. When we do it right, we can turn them on to the things we
believe. But when we do it wrong, we can turn them off to the values
we most hope they will embrace. The goal is to find ways of making
this reality work for us, rather than against us. How? By creating
and capturing opportunities to impress upon the next generation
our values and beliefs. In other words, through what we've labeled
impression points.

The kids are all standing at the foot of the stairs. Jim is at the top
of that same staircase. They wait eagerly for Dad's instructions.

"I'll take you to Baskin Robbins for ice cream if you can figure
how to get up here." He has the attention of all four kids. "But there
are a few rules. First, you can't touch the stairs. Second, you can't
touch the railing. Now, begin!"

After several contemplative moments, the youngest speaks up.
"That's impossible, Dad! How can we get to where you are without

touching the stairs or the railing?"

After some disgruntled agreement from two of the other children, Jacob gets an idea. "Hey, Dad. Come down here." Jim walks down the stairs. "Now bend over while I get on your back. Okay, climb the stairs."

Bingo! Jim proceeds to parallel this simple game with how it is impossible to get to God on our own. But when we trust Christ's completed work on our behalf, we can get to heaven. A lasting impression is made. After a trip up the stairs on Dad's back, the whole gang piles into the minivan for a double scoop of mint-chip.

Six years ago, Jim and his wife Janet began setting aside time to intentionally impress upon the kids their values and beliefs through a weekly ritual called "family night." They play games, talk, study, and do the things which reinforce the importance of family and faith. It is during these times that they intentionally create these impression points with their kids. The impact? The kids are having fun and a heritage is being passed.

☙ intentional or "oops"?

Sometimes, we accidentally impress the wrong things on our kids rather than intentionally impressing the right things. But there is an effective, easy way to change that. Routine family nights are a powerful tool for creating intentional impression points with our children.

The concept behind family nights is rooted in a biblical mandate summarized in Deuteronomy 6:5-9.

> *"Love the Lord your God with all your heart and with all your soul and with all your strength. These commandments that I give you today are to be upon your hearts. Impress them on your children."*
> *How?*
> *"Talk about them when you sit at home and when you walk along the road, when you lie down and when you get up. Tie them as symbols on your hands and bind them on your foreheads. Write them on the doorframes of your houses and on your gates."*

In other words, we need to take advantage of every opportunity to impress our beliefs and values in the lives of our children. A growing network of parents are discovering family nights to be a highly effective, user-friendly approach to doing just that. As one father put it ,"This has changed our entire family life." And another dad, "Our investment of time and energy into family nights has more eternal value than we may ever know." Why? Because they are intentionally teaching their children at the wisdom level, the level at which the children understand and can apply eternal truths.

◉ truth is a treasure

Two boys are running all over the house, carefully following the complex and challenging instructions spelled out on the "truth treasure map" they received moments ago. An earlier map contained a few rather simple instructions that were much easier to follow. But the "false treasure box" it lead to left something to be desired. It was empty. Boo Dad! They hope for a better result with map number two.

STEP ONE:

Walk sixteen paces into the front family room.

STEP TWO:

Spin around seven times, then walk down the stairs.

STEP THREE:

Run backwards to the other side of the room.

STEP FOUR:

Try and get around Dad and climb under the table.

You get the picture. The boys are laughing at themselves, complaining to Dad, and having a ball. After twenty minutes of treasure hunting they finally reach the elusive "truth treasure box." Little hands open the lid, hoping for a better result this time around. They aren't disappointed. The box contains a nice selection of their favorite candies. Yea Dad!

"Which map was easier to follow?" Dad asks.

"The first one," comes their response.

"Which one was better?"

"The second one. It led to a true treasure," says the oldest.

"That's just like life," Dad shares. "Sometimes it's easier to follow what is false. But it is always better to seek and follow what is true."

They read from Proverbs 2 about the hidden treasure of God's truth and end their time repeating tonight's jingle—"It's best for you to seek what's true." Then they indulge themselves with a mouthful of delicious candy!

☙ the power of family nights

The power of family nights is twofold. First, it creates a formal setting within which Dad and Mom can intentionally instill beliefs, values, or character qualities within their child. Rather than defer to the influence of peers and media, or abdicate character training to the school and church, parents create the opportunity to teach their children the things that matter most.

The second impact of family nights is perhaps even more significant than the first. Twenty to sixty minutes of formal fun and instruction can set up countless opportunities for informal reinforcement. These informal impression points do not have to be created, they just happen—at the dinner table, while driving in the car, while watching television, or any other parent/child time together. Once you have formally discussed a given family night topic, you and your children will naturally refer back to those principles during the routine dialogues of everyday life.

If the truth were known, many of us hated family devotions while growing up. We had them sporadically at best, usually whenever our parents were feeling particularly guilty. But that was fine, since the only thing worse was a trip to the dentist. Honestly, do we really think that is what God had in mind when He instructed us to teach our children? As an alternative, many parents are discovering family nights to be a wonderful complement to or replacement for family devotions as a means of passing their beliefs and values to the kids. In fact, many parents hear their kids ask at least three times per week:

"Can we have family night tonight?"

Music to Dad's and Mom's ears!

Keys to Effective Family Nights

There are several keys which should be incorporated into effective family nights.

MAKE IT FUN!

Enjoy yourself, and let the kids have a ball. They may not remember everything you say, but they will always cherish the times of laughter—and so will you.

KEEP IT SIMPLE!

The minute you become sophisticated or complicated, you've missed the whole point. Don't try to create deeply profound lessons. Just try to reinforce your values and beliefs in a simple, easy-to-understand manner. Read short passages, not long, drawn-out sections of Scripture. Remember: The goal is to keep it simple.

DON'T DOMINATE!

You want to pull them into the discovery process as much as possible. If you do all the talking, you've missed the mark. Ask questions, give assignments, invite participation in every way possible. They will learn more when you involve all of their senses and emotions.

GO WITH THE FLOW!

It's fine to start with a well-defined outline, but don't kill spontaneity by becoming overly structured. If an incident or question leads you in a different direction, great! Some of the best impression opportunities are completely unplanned and unexpected.

MIX IT UP!

Don't allow yourself to get into a rut or routine. Keep the sense of excitement and anticipation through variety. Experiment to discover what works best for your family. Use books, games, videos, props, made-up stories, songs, music or music videos, or even go on a family outing.

DO IT OFTEN!

We tend to find time for the things that are really important. It is best to set aside one evening per week (the same evening if possible) for family night. Remember, repetition is the best teacher. The more impressions you can create, the more of an impact you will make.

MAKE A MEMORY!

Find ways to make the lesson stick. For example, just as advertisers create "jingles" to help us remember their products, it is helpful to create family night "jingles" to remember the main theme—such as "It's best for you to seek what's true" or "Just like air, God is there!"

USE OTHER TOOLS FROM THE HERITAGE BUILDERS TOOL CHEST!

Family night is only one exciting way for you to intentionally build a loving heritage for your family. You'll also want to use these other exciting tools from Heritage Builders.

The Family Fragrance: There are five key qualities to a healthy family fragrance, each contributing to an environment of love in the home. It's easy to remember the Fragrance Five by fitting them into an acrostic using the word "Aroma"—

A—Affection
R—Respect
O—Order
M—Merriment
A—Affirmation

Impression Points: Ways that we impress on our children our values, preferences, and concerns. We do it through our talk and our actions. We do it intentionally (through such methods as Family Nights), and we do it incidentally.

The Right Angle: The Right Angle is the standard of normal healthy living against which our children will be able to measure their atttitudes, actions, and beliefs.

Traditions: Meaningful activities which the process of passing on emotional, spiritual, and relational inheritance between generations. Family traditions can play a vital role in this process.

Please see the back of the book for information on how to receive the FREE Heritage Builders Newsletter which contains more information about these exciting tools! Also, look for the new book, *The Heritage,* available at your local Christian bookstore.

@ How to Use This Tool Chest

Summary page: For those who like the bottom line, we have provided a summary sheet at the start of each family night session. This abbreviated version of the topic briefly highlights the goal, key Scriptures, activity overview, main points, and life slogan. On the reverse side of this detachable page there is space provided for you to write down any ideas you wish to add or alter as you make the lesson your own.

Step-by-step: For those seeking suggestions and directions for each step in the family night process, we have provided a section which walks you through every activity, question, Scripture reading, and discussion point. Feel free to follow each step as written as you conduct the session, or read through this portion in preparation for your time together.

À la carte: We strongly encourage you to use the material in this book in an "à la carte" manner. In other words, pick and choose the questions, activities, Scriptures, age-appropriate ideas, etc. which best fit your family. This book is not intended to serve as a curriculum, requiring compliance with our sequence and plan, but rather as a tool chest from which you can grab what works for you and which can be altered to fit your family situation.

The long and the short of it: Each family night topic presented in this book includes several activities, related Scriptures, and possible discussion items. Do not feel it is necessary to conduct them all in a single family night. You may wish to spread one topic over several weeks using smaller portions of each chapter, depending upon the attention span of the kids and the energy level of the parents. Remember, short and effective is better than long and thorough.

Journaling: Finally, we have provided space with each session for you to capture a record of meaningful comments, funny happenings, and unplanned moments which will inevitably occur during family night. Keep a notebook of these journal entries for future reference. You will treasure this permanent record of the heritage passing process for years to come.

⊙ 1: Are You Satisfied?

Exploring what it means to be content

Scripture
- Luke 12:13-21—The Parable of the Rich Fool.
- Philippians 4:11-13—Being content with little or much.
- 1 Timothy 6:7-8—Contentment with food and clothing.

ACTIVITY OVERVIEW		
Activity	**Summary**	**Pre-Session Prep**
Activity 1: Mine!	Children try to keep as much candy as possible in this game.	You'll need a Bible, a timer with a buzzer, a large bowl of small candies, and a smaller bowl for each child in your family.
Activity 2: How Much Do I Need?	Evaluate needs versus wants.	You'll need a Bible and a candle.
Activity 3: My Favorite	Discuss feelings toward favorite possessions.	You'll need no supplies. A box is optional.

Main Points:

—God gives us all we have, and God can take it away.

—We can be content with a lot or a little.

—We all place too high a value on our possessions.

LIFE SLOGAN: "Be content with what God sent."

Make it your own
In the space provided below, outline the flow and add any additional ideas
to guide you through the process of conducting this family night.

Prayer & Praise Items
In the space provided below, list any items you wish to pray about or give
praise for during this family night session.

Journal
In the space provided below, capture a record of any fun or meaningful
things which happened during this family night session.

Session Tip

We intentionally have provided more material than we would expect to be used in a single "Family Night" session. You know your family's unique interests and life circumstances best, so feel free to adapt this session to meet your family members' needs. Remember, short and simple is better than long and comprehensive.

 WARM-UP

Open with Prayer: Begin by having a family member pray, asking God to help everyone in the family understand more about Him through this time. After prayer, review your last lesson by asking these questions:

- **What do you remember from our last lesson?**
- **Do you remember the Life Slogan?**
- **What was one fun thing we did during our last lesson?**
- **How has what we learned last week changed your actions in the past few days?**

Share: Today we're going to be learning about what contentment is.

ACTIVITY 1: Mine!

Point: God gives us all we have, and God can take it away.

 **Supplies:** You'll need a Bible, a timer with a bell or buzzer, a large bowl of small candies (such as M&Ms) and a smaller bowl for each child in your family. (*Note:* If you're concerned about your children having too much candy, use other items, such as pennies, stickers, or other small items your children will be ready to grab.)

Activity: Place the large bowl of candy in the center of your living room. Give each child a smaller bowl. Have the children put the bowls on their beds and then return to you.

Share: When I say "Go," you may pick up one piece of candy, run to your bowl and drop the candy in, then run back for another. Don't eat

any now, just take one candy at a time to your bowl. Now here's the tricky part. I'm going to set the timer. You won't know how long I've set it for. If you're touching your bowl, while it's on your bed, at the exact second that the timer goes off, you can keep all the candy in your bowl. But if you're not touching the bowl, you'll have to give up the candy.

Set the timer (without letting children see the amount of time) and begin the activity. Children may seem to hover about their bowls and rush about to get the candy, but let them do what seems best to them. When the timer goes off, call out "Freeze" to ensure that your children don't try to rush to their bowls in an attempt to save their candy. Have those who were not at their bowls pour the candy they'd gathered back into the larger bowl in the living room. Have any children who were at their bowls bring the bowls with them back to the living room, but don't allow them to eat any of the candy yet.

Gather everyone around to discuss:
- **What did you like or not like about this activity?**
- **Do you think this is a fair game? Why or why not?**
- **Is it easy or hard for you to be happy for someone who gets to keep the candy? Explain your answer.**
- **Who gave you the candy?**
- **Why do you feel like it's not fair for me to take away the candy?**

Share: To help us think more about what's happened here, I want to read a story from the Bible.

Read Luke 12:13-21 aloud, then discuss:
- **What happened in this story?** (A rich man had a large crop and wanted to keep it all. He tore down his old barns, built new ones, and figured he'd have any easy life from then on. Unfortunately, he died that night, and all he had was useless to him.)
- **What do you think Jesus wants us to learn from this story?** (Not to be greedy; that no things last forever; we shouldn't put our faith in money or things we own.)
- **What does this story have to do with our game with the candy?**

Share: We can learn several things from this game and from the story

Jesus told. First, we shouldn't be greedy. When we were playing the game, each person was concerned about getting enough candy for himself or herself. In life, people are concerned about gathering material possessions, instead of with their relationship with God. Second, just as God gave the rich man a big crop and took it away, so God can give to us and take away from us. It's not up to us to say what's fair. God wants us to be thankful for what we have, but also to trust in Him instead of trusting in what we have. Everything we have we got from God, and God can take these things away from us too.

After your discussion, allow children who were able to keep their candy to eat it (or at least some of it). Then explain that, because you love your children, you'll let those who had to give back their candy each take one handful.

ACTIVITY 2: How Much Do I Need?

Point: We can be content with a lot or a little.

Supplies: You'll need a Bible and a candle.

Activity: Create a sense of what the Apostle Paul experienced by bringing the family into a dark portion of the house, perhaps a closet or corner of the basement. Explain that Paul wrote some important things about contentment while in a dark, lonely prison. Light a candle for a reading light.

Share: Paul, who was originally named Saul, was a rich and privileged man. He went to school in a time when few people were educated. He was part of a group of religious leaders who hated the Christians. In fact, he hunted down some of the first Christians to be sure they were killed. So Paul knew what it was like to be rich and have plenty of food and things.
     Then, through an encounter with God, Paul became a Christian himself! Suddenly he was the one being hunted and put into jail. He had to endure hunger, cold, and rejection.
- **How would you have responded to this? Would you have told God, "No fair"?**

Age Adjustments

Further your discussion with OLDER CHILDREN AND TEENAGERS by talking about situations in your lives and the world that seem unfair. Why do some people have plenty of money, food, possessions, or love when others have very little or none? Do you ever feel greedy when you want more and more? What do you think God wants you to do about this? What do you think God wants you to learn from these situations? How have you learned to be content at a time when you had less than others?

Teenagers may also learn more about this topic by reading the Book of Job. How did Job respond when God took away his riches, his family, and his health? What can we learn from Job, his friends, and Job's relationship with God?

• Have you ever done what you knew was the right thing, what God wanted you to do, but you still were punished or had things go wrong for you? If so, tell about that time.

Share: Well, let's find out how Paul responded to this seemingly unfair situation. And before I read this, I want you to know that Paul wrote this while he was in jail.

 Read Philippians 4:11-13 aloud, then discuss:
• **What does Paul's attitude here seem to be?** (He's content; he's relying on God for strength, not on what he has.)
• **Could you say these things if you were in prison?**

Share: Let's read more of what Paul had to say about being content.

 Read 1 Timothy 6:7-8 together, then discuss:
• **What is the message of these verses?** (We should be content if we have food and clothing, and not want more; we were born without anything, and won't be able to take anything with us when we die.)
• **Do you feel like you're able to be content with food and clothing? What do you think is also necessary for you to be content?**
• **What are things you should be trying to do instead of getting more new toys, new cars, nicer furniture, and so on?** (We should be trying to show God's love to others; we should be trying to obey the Bible; we should be trying to help others.)

ACTIVITY 3: My Favorite

Point: We all place too high a value on our possessions.

 Supplies: You'll need no supplies for this activity. A box is optional.

Activity: Ask each family member, including yourself, to go and get a favorite possession or two and bring them back to a central place—perhaps a large box in the family room. (Depending upon each person's age, the possession could be a favorite book, stuffed animal, music CD, Gameboy, or laptop computer.)

Ask each person to share what he or she likes about the possession(s) chosen, and how they would react if that item were stolen, lost, or destroyed.

Share: It is normal for us to like our possessions. This can be good because it makes us want to take care of them. But if those possessions become more important to us than they should, we can have problems.

Discuss this question:
• **What are some of the problems that come when we become too attached to our things?** (We develop selfish attitudes; our priorities get messed up; we don't want to give to those in need; etc.)

WRAP-UP

Gather everyone in a circle and have family members take turns answering this question: **What's one thing you've learned about God today?**

Next, tell kids you've got a new "Life Slogan" you'd like to share with them.

Age Adjustments

If allowed in your city, take OLDER CHILDREN OR TEENAGERS to a nearby prison, homeless shelter, or other area where people are in want. How can you help these people? How could you learn to be content if you were in their situation? How does learning more about those in need help you to be more thankful for what you have?

Life Slogan: Today's Life Slogan is this: "Be content with what God sent." Have family members repeat the slogan two or three times to help them learn it. Then encourage them to practice saying it during the week so they can talk about it at your next family night session.

Close in Prayer: Allow time for each family member to share prayer concerns and answers to prayer. Then close your time together with prayer for each concern. Thank God for making families, especially your family! Take time to thank God for each family member, mentioning one special quality you're thankful for about that person.

Remember to record prayer requests here so you can refer to them in the future as you see God answering them.

Additional Resources:

Bible Words About Happiness by Lois Rock (ages 4–7)
Money Matters
Money Matters for Kids Board Game (ages 6–10)
Financial Parenting by Larry Burkett
The Chosen Ones by Janet Holm McHenry (ages 8–12)
A Better Tomorrow? by Dorothy Harrison (ages 8–12)

2: Lock the Gate!

Exploring the importance of controlling our thoughts

Scripture
• Proverbs 4:23—Guard your heart.
• 2 Corinthians 11:3—Bad thoughts lead us away from God.
• Philippians 4:8—List of what God *does* want us to think about.
• Psalm 119:9, 11—We keep our minds pure by filling them with God's Word.

ACTIVITY OVERVIEW

Activity	Summary	Pre-Session Prep
Activity 1: Garbage In, Garbage Out	Evaluate the thoughts we let into our minds.	You'll need a Bible, a large piece of poster board for each family member, a stack of old magazines, glue, scissors, and markers.
Activity 2: Make Room for Me!	See how bad thoughts push out good thoughts, and vice versa.	You'll need a Bible, a bucket of water, and several large rocks.

Main Points:

—We must guard the gates to our minds.

—Fill your mind with good so there won't be room for the bad.

LIFE SLOGAN: "To stay out of a bind, let God control your mind."

Make it your own
In the space provided below, outline the flow and add any additional ideas to guide you through the process of conducting this family night.

Prayer & Praise Items
In the space provided below, list any items you wish to pray about or give praise for during this family night session.

Journal
In the space provided below, capture a record of any fun or meaningful things which happened during this family night session.

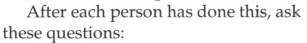
Session Tip

We intentionally have provided more material than we would expect to be used in a single "Family Night" session. You know your family's unique interests and life circumstances best, so feel free to adapt this lesson to meet your family members' needs. Remember, short and simple is better than long and comprehensive.

 WARM-UP

Open with Prayer: Begin by having a family member pray, asking God to help everyone in the family understand more about Him through this time. After prayer, review your last lesson by asking these questions:

- **What do you remember from our last lesson?**
- **Do you remember the Life Slogan?**
- **What was one fun thing we did during our last lesson?**
- **How has what we learned last week changed your actions in the past few days?**

Share: Today we're going to learn about why it's important to control our thoughts, and how to do that!

ACTIVITY 1: Garbage In, Garbage Out

Point: We must guard the gates to our minds.

 Supplies: You'll need a Bible, a large piece of poster board for each family member, a stack of old magazines, glue, scissors, and markers.

Activity: Give each family member a piece of poster board or a large sheet of paper.

Explain: **Draw a picture of your face in the center of the poster.**

After each person has done this, ask these questions:

- **Where is your mind in the picture?** (In the brain; you can't see it.)
- **How do thoughts get into our minds?**

Share: Thoughts get into our minds often through our ears and eyes. They could also get into our minds through our mouths, noses, or even our bodies by our actions. We can consider these parts of our bodies the gates to our thoughts. Let's add more to our pictures by including thoughts that are trying to get through these gates and into our minds.

Using the magazines and craft supplies, have family members look for pictures of things they're likely to see, hear, smell, or taste on an average day. These pictures can be cut out and glued to the appropriate person's picture with an arrow showing how it gets into that person's mind. For example, a picture of chocolate cake could have arrows pointing to the mouth. If a picture of a typical thought can't be found, family members can draw their own pictures or write a word or two on their drawing. Encourage family members to think of things they're likely to really encounter in their lives. Also remember to be honest—all thoughts might not be good!

If your family seems unsure as to what they should include, suggest some of these ideas to get them started:

Eyes: pictures of friends, family members, school; the names of television shows and movies often watched; a picture of a computer or video game.

Ears: names of songs you like; pictures of birds; names of friends you often talk with.

Nose: pictures of flowers or food.

Mouth: pictures of food, drinks, medicines, cigarettes.

When each person has several "thought pictures" added to their original drawing, take turns explaining your pictures. Then discuss the following questions:

- **Which thoughts can get in by more than one gate?** (A movie we both see and hear; food we taste and smell.)
- **Which pictures have you included to show where good thoughts come from?**
- **Which pictures have you included to show where bad thoughts come from?**

Share: God is very concerned about our thoughts. Let me read some verses from the Bible so we can learn more about this.

Read Proverbs 4:23 and 2 Corinthians 11:3, then discuss:
- **Why should we guard our hearts or our thoughts?** (Because they are the wellspring of life; because our thoughts help determine what our actions will be.)

- **How can we guard our thoughts?** (By guarding the gates to our minds; by not watching certain movies or shows; by choosing carefully the music we listen to.)

- **Why is God so concerned about our thoughts?** (Because He doesn't want us to be lead away from Him; God wants our thoughts to be on Him; if our thoughts are bad, our actions might be bad too.)

- **What do you think God wants us to think about, and why?** (Good things, because then we're more likely to do good things; God wants us to think about Him so we'll be more like Him.)

Age Adjustments

YOUNGER CHILDREN are less likely to have many pictures of bad thoughts as you've most likely guarded what they see, hear, do, and so on. But this is a good chance to help them understand why you sometimes keep them from certain activities. However, to make this activity easier for very young children, focus only on the eyes and ears and keep the "thought pictures" to just a few. For example, if they hear a bad word, then the word is in their minds and they might think about it and later say it themselves. The same is true of a good word. Or if they see a movie with a scary part, that will become a thought in their minds and might later return in a bad dream. But a movie showing someone being kind might help them remember to be kind, or a show with something funny might make them laugh when they remember that thought later!

Encourage OLDER CHILDREN AND TEENAGERS to use Philippians 4:8 to rate the kinds of movies and shows they watch, the music they listen to, their conversations with their friends, and so on. To clearly help your teen or older child do this, choose a movie or television show your older child or teenager likes to watch but you feel is a negative influence. Watch five or ten minutes of this show together, then see if you can find anything in this show true, noble, right, pure, lovely, and so on as listed in Philippians 4:8. How does the show rate?

Repeat this with several popular songs from your child's favorite radio station or CD. Also rate the way certain friends talk. Do these conversations encourage you to be more like God or more sinful? How are the thoughts you're allowing through the gates of your mind changing your words, attitudes, and actions?

Parents, beware! Your children are likely to call you on this as well. Are *you* letting the right thoughts into *your* gates? Be ready to be held accountable by your kids.

Read Philippians 4:8 and discuss:

- **Which things on your picture fit the Bible's description of what we should be thinking about?**
- **What things should be going into the gates of your mind so your thoughts will be the thoughts God desires for you?**
- **How will putting these thoughts into our minds change our actions?** (Good thoughts will lead to good actions, while bad thoughts will lead to bad actions.)

Share: When you're young, you haven't learned enough about choosing what to allow through the gates of your mind. That's why I sometimes choose the shows you'll watch, the songs you can listen to, or even the friends you can play with. God holds me responsible for the thoughts I allow to go into your gates until you're old enough to choose for yourself.

ACTIVITY 2: Make Room for Me!

Point: Fill your mind with good so there won't be room for the bad.

 Supplies: You'll need a Bible, a bucket of water, and several large rocks. This activity will spill water, so consider doing it outside or in the sink.

Activity: Fill the bucket to the brim with water. Have one of the children read Philippians 4:8 again.

Share: This bucket represents our minds. Let's say the water is all the good thoughts we've just read about in the Bible—the excellent, lovely, pure things of God. What might some of those thoughts be? (Answers will widely vary, but could include words from the Bible, the voices of those we love, laughter, memories of beautiful scenery or fun outings, and so on.)

Share: Now we have these rocks. These represent the bad thoughts Satan wants to put in our minds.

Before you drop each rock into the water, have your children think of a bad thought to associate with that rock. For example, one rock might represent *hit your brother*, another might be *smoke ciga-rettes*, and another might be *steal this piece of candy*. The seriousness of the thoughts will vary depending upon the ages of your children.

Drop the rocks one at a time into the water, saying out loud the bad thought represented by that rock. Watch as the water spills out. When all the rocks have been used, discuss:

- **What happened to the good thoughts?** (They spilled out to make room for the bad thoughts.)
- **How is this activity with the water like the thoughts that really go into our minds?** (The bad thoughts push out the good thoughts; the bad thoughts can fill up our minds.)
- **How can we use this same idea to get rid of bad thoughts?** (Push out bad thoughts by putting more good thoughts into our minds.)

Share: When we let bad thoughts into our minds, we start to push out the good thoughts. But if we focus on God and the good thoughts He wants in our minds, we won't leave any room for the bad thoughts to come in. The Bible explains this clearly.

 Read Psalm 119:9 and 11 aloud.

Share: We keep our actions pure, or in line with God's desires, by living by the Bible. God says the more Bible verses we "hide in our hearts," the less we'll sin. Why do you think this is true? (The more we remember the Bible, or God's instruction, the more we'll know what's wrong and not want to do it; by only thinking about God and good thoughts, we won't have time or the desire to think or do wrong things.)

Age Adjustments

FOR ALL AGES, this might be a good time to suggest Scripture memorization to your children. Choose verses according to the ages of your children, and think of fun ways to learn them together. Thus you'll all be hiding God's Word in your hearts together.

 WRAP-UP

Gather everyone in a circle and have family members take turns answering this question: **What's one thing you've learned about God today?**

Next, tell kids you've got a new "Life Slogan" you'd like to share with them.

Life Slogan: Today's Life Slogan is this: "To stay out of a bind, let God control your mind." Have family members repeat the slogan two or three times to help them learn it. Then encourage them to practice saying it during the week so they can talk about it at your next family night session.

Close in Prayer: Allow time for each family member to share prayer concerns and answers to prayer. Then close your time together with prayer for each concern. Thank God for making families, especially your family! Take time to thank God for each family member, mentioning one special quality you're thankful for about that person.

Remember to record prayer requests here so you can refer to them in the future as you see God answering them.

Additional Resources:

The Family Book of Christian Values by Stuart and Jill Briscoe
Tales of Faith & Wonder by Hans Christian Andersen (ages 4–12)
A Feast of Good Stories by Pat Alexander

28

@ 3: No Mission Impossible

Exploring God's view of the impossible

Scripture
• John 6:1-14—Jesus feeds the five thousand.
• Jeremiah 32:17—Nothing is too hard for God.
• Luke 18:27—What's impossible for people is possible for God.

ACTIVITY OVERVIEW		
Activity	Summary	Pre-Session Prep
Activity 1: God Can Do It	See that God has the power to solve our problems.	You'll need a Bible, a sturdy plank of wood, a brick, and a snack of fish and crackers.
Activity 2: The Informant	Understand God's view of problems compared to our view.	You'll need a Bible and a card game or deck of cards.

Main Points:

—God can do what we think is impossible.

—Difficult situations can help us grow.

LIFE SLOGAN: "Though hard for you, there's nothing God can't do!"

Make it your own
In the space provided below, outline the flow and add any additional ideas to guide you through the process of conducting this family night.

Prayer & Praise Items
In the space provided below, list any items you wish to pray about or give praise for during this family night session.

Journal
In the space provided below, capture a record of any fun or meaningful things which happened during this family night session.

WARM-UP

Open with Prayer: Begin by having a family member pray, asking God to help everyone in the family understand more about Him through this time. After prayer, review your last lesson by asking these questions:

- **What do you remember from our last lesson?**
- **Do you remember the Life Slogan?**
- **What was one fun thing we did during our last lesson?**
- **How has what we learned last week changed your actions in the past few days?**

Share: During our family time today we'll be discovering how to face tough situations.

ACTIVITY 1: God Can Do It

Point: God can do what we think is impossible.

Supplies: You'll need a Bible, a sturdy plank of wood (six or more inches wide and six to eight feet long), a brick or other object to use as a fulcrum, and a snack of fish (tuna, sardines, or fish crackers), and crackers.

Activity: Ask your children if any of them think they can lift you off the ground. Let any volunteers make attempts, until they've all agreed they can't do it. Then bring out the plank of wood. Place the brick or other object under the plank as a fulcrum. Stand on one end of the

Age Adjustments

YOUNGER CHILDREN might also get a kick out of the challenge to pick up your family car. After a few attempts, show them how to use a jack to easily lift the car. What seemed impossible turned out to be easy with the right equipment, and what seems hard for us is easy for God. He's always got the right equipment!

Also for younger children, help them visualize how many people 5,000 really is. Think of places your child has been and can imagine full of people. For example, "That's more people than are in our whole church!" Or "Remember when we went to that basketball game? That was about 5,000 people. Can you imagine a few fish and a few loaves of bread feeding all those people?"

FOR OLDER CHILDREN OR TEENS, the challenge to lift you might not be much of a challenge. If your kids are bigger than you, change the challenge to you lifting them, or one of them lifting another. You could also change the challenge so they lift a large object instead of a person.

plank and have one of your children stand on the other end. Adjust the fulcrum until your child's weight is enough to lift your end of the plank off the ground. Let all your children take turns at this, seeing how easy it is to lift you with the right equipment.

Discuss:

- **What are things that used to seem hard for you?** (Answers may include riding a bike, tying shoes, reading, and so on.)
- **Why are these things easy for you now?** (I've grown; I've learned to do more.)
- **What are things to which you would say "I can't" if you're asked to do them?** (Answers might include driving a car, repairing a television, teaching my class at school.)

Share: Some things we become able to do as we grow and mature. But there still might be times we're faced with a situation and we say, "I can't do that!" Listen to this story of a situation where this happened in the Bible.

Read John 6:1-14 aloud. After reading the story, discuss:

- **What happened at the beginning of this story?** (A crowd of people followed Jesus to hear Him and be healed. As time went by, the people became hungry.)
- **What was the problem?** (There was only a tiny amount of food available. To buy food for everyone would cost as much as a man would earn in eight months.)

Bring out the fish and crackers to snack on. As your kids start to eat, explain that the fish the people ate on that day would have been small fish and that the bread would have been hard bread.

- **What was the attitude of Jesus' disciples?** (We can't do this!)
- **What was Jesus' attitude?** (God can do this!)
- **How is this story like you trying to pick me up?** (We didn't think we could do it, but we could after all. What looked hard turned out to be easier than we thought it could be.)
- **How can hearing this story help us have a different attitude toward problems?** (We know we can turn to God for help; we can pray that if God wants this problem to be changed, He'll change it or give us the ideas or abilities to change it.)

Share: Jesus thanked God for that little amount of fish and bread, then He broke it again—and again and again and again—until there was enough to feed more than five thousand people! In a situation where we would say "I can't do it!" God says, *"I can do it!"*

ACTIVITY 2: The Informant

Point: Difficult situations can help us grow.

 Supplies: You'll need a Bible and a deck of game cards such as Old Maid, or use a regular deck for Crazy Eights.

Only One Child?
If you're playing with just you and one child, simply let your child see your cards whenever he or she wants!

Activity: Explain that you'll all play a game of Old Maid or Crazy Eights for younger kids, or perhaps Battleship or Uno for older kids. But before you deal the cards, have your oldest child stand behind your youngest child. Deal the cards to everyone except the oldest child. Then, before playing, explain that the oldest child will be able to roam about the playing area and look at everyone else's cards. This child can then whisper information gathered from looking at other cards into the ear of the youngest child. The youngest child can listen to or ignore the information as he or she chooses. Despite any protests from other children, begin playing.

Obviously, the child with help will be at an advantage in the game. If the game ends quickly, let another child be the informant for a sibling. Play as long as your children like, then gather the cards and discuss:

- **What made it easy to win if you were listening to the informant?** (You knew what cards other people had.)
- **Why did you trust the person giving you information?** (He could see what I couldn't see; she told me what other people were going to do.)
- **How is this game like turning to God in tough situations?** (God can see what I can't see; God knows the answers even though I don't.)
- **How does God give us information to know what to do in these situations?** (Mostly through the Bible.)
- **What do you think this means for your life?** (I should be reading the Bible more; I should look to God for direction, instead of to myself or others.)

Read Jeremiah 32:17 and Luke 18:27 aloud, then discuss:
- **What are the main messages of these verses?** (Nothing is

too hard for God; even if something seems impossible to us, it's possible for God.)

- **How do these verses make you feel about facing difficult situations?** (God can help me; God can do what I can't do.)
- **How do these verses relate to our game?** (Even when I was dealt a bad hand, I had help to win; God sees what we don't see and helps us get through difficult situations.)

Share: Sometimes God gives us a challenge, a test, or a difficult situation, just as it looked difficult to pick me up, or you thought you wouldn't win at the game, or the disciples thought they wouldn't be able to feed all those people. But when we trust God, and then God presents a way to solve the problem, we learn more about God and grow from the experience. Sometimes the test looks so hard we forget to look to God. We have to remember that God knows everything, and God is powerful enough to solve any problem. He knows the beginning and the end!

WRAP-UP

Gather everyone in a circle and have family members take turns answering this question: **What's one thing you've learned about God today?**

Next, tell kids you've got a new "Life Slogan" you'd like to share with them.

Life Slogan: Today's Life Slogan is this: "Though hard for you, there's nothing God can't do!" Have family members repeat the slogan two or three times to help them learn it. Then encourage them to practice saying it during the week so they can talk about it at your next family night session.

Close in Prayer: Allow time for each family member to share prayer concerns and answers to prayer. Then close your time together with prayer for each concern. Thank God for making families, especially your family! Take time to thank God for each family member, mentioning one special quality you're thankful for about that person.

Remember to record prayer requests here so you can refer to them in the future as you see God answering them.

Additional Resources:

Operation Morningstar by Dorothy Harrison (ages 8–12)
Looking for Home by Arleta Richardson (ages 8–12)

@ 4: Worrywart

Exploring how God wants us to respond to our worries

Scripture
- Matthew 6:25-34—Just as God cares for the birds and flowers, He'll care for us.
- Philippians 4:6-7—Be anxious for nothing.
- Psalm 55:22—Cast your cares before God.

ACTIVITY OVERVIEW		
Activity	Summary	Pre-Session Prep
Activity 1: That's Shocking!	Experience anxiety as a potential shock.	You'll need a board, an inexpensive doorbell buzzer, a 9-volt battery, an extra length of electrical wire, and a large bolt, plus assorted tools.
Activity 2: No Worries	Explore God's answer to worries.	You'll need a Bible, paper, and pencils.

Main Points:

—Worrying doesn't change anything.

—God doesn't want us to worry about anything.

LIFE SLOGAN: "Don't worry. Pray and be happy."

Make it your own
In the space provided below, outline the flow and add any additional ideas to guide you through the process of conducting this family night.

Prayer & Praise Items
In the space provided below, list any items you wish to pray about or give praise for during this family night session.

Journal
In the space provided below, capture a record of any fun or meaningful things which happened during this family night session.

WARM-UP

Open with Prayer: Begin by having a family member pray, asking God to help everyone in the family understand more about Him through this time. After prayer, review your last lesson by asking these questions:

- **What do you remember from our last lesson?**
- **Do you remember the Life Slogan?**
- **What was one fun thing we did during our last lesson?**
- **How has what we learned last week changed your actions in the past few days?**

Share: Today we'll learn why worrying doesn't help us.

ACTIVITY 1: That's Shocking!

Point: Worrying doesn't change anything.

 Supplies: The preparation for this activity is a little more complicated than normal, but it has a great effect, so it's worth it all! You'll need a board of any size, an inexpensive doorbell (from the hardware store), a 9-volt battery, an extra length of electrical wire, and a large bolt. You'll also probably need a few tools, such as screwdrivers and a hammer.

Activity: Prepare for this activity well in advance so you have time to get it all in place. Doorbell buzzers are usually attached to an electrical supply, but many will work with a battery as well. Remove the doorbell from its packaging and mount it onto a board. Attach one of the wires from the doorbell to the battery. Leave the other one hanging free. Take the extra length of electrical wire and place one end under the doorbell mechanism so it looks attached but actually isn't. This is the "dummy" wire. Leave the other end of the dummy wire hanging free as well. Screw the large bolt into the board at any spot.

Just so you know, the dummy wire and the bolt have nothing to do with the doorbell working. However, don't let your kids know this!

Now test your work. When you touch the extra active wire to the battery, the doorbell should buzz or ring. You may need to touch the wires and press the button on the doorbell as well. Check your wires and consult with any directions that came along with the doorbell. When you've got it down so that the doorbell rings when you touch the active wire to the battery, your contraption is ready!

Ask at your hardware store for a buzzer powered by a battery.

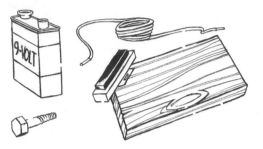

Also, prepare another family member (preferably an adult) to go first in testing your experiment. This person will need to pretend to feel a quick and painful shock.

Gather family members together and let everyone see your handiwork.

Explain: **I need to test this buzzer and see if it works. I'm going to have Mom help me.**

Have Mom (or whoever is in on this with you) place one hand on the bolt and one hand on the dummy wire.

Explain: **Now I'm going to touch this wire (the active wire) to the battery and see if the buzzer works.**

Touch the wires, and when the buzzer sounds, Mom should jump or otherwise react as if she's been shocked.

Share: Well, it worked! Sorry about Mom getting shocked, but my buzzer works. Now I want everyone else to take a turn holding the wire and the bolt.

If your children are afraid and refuse to participate, don't force them. If anyone volunteers, have him or her repeat the steps Mom took. To add to the anticipation, hesitate a second or two before touching the wires together, or have your child close his or her eyes.

Obviously, the child will hear the buzzer but won't feel a thing. If you have more children waiting to take a turn, explain that something must have gone wrong for the first child to not get shocked. Have Mom try again, fake being shocked, then ask for the second child to try it. Continue until all the children who want to have participated.

Share: Okay, I'll let you in on the trick. This wire you were holding doesn't do anything! Mom was faking it all along!

Show children that the wire isn't actually attached, then ask:
- **Were you worried about being shocked? What did you think it would feel like?**
- **Even though you were worried, what happened?** (Nothing! I was worried for no reason.)
- **Have you ever worried about something, like thinking I'd been in a car accident when I was late to pick you up or something like that, and then found out everything was okay and you'd worried for nothing? Tell about that time.**

Share: Sometimes we worry about things for no reason. Just like the shock and the buzzer, there was nothing to worry about in reality. Worrying doesn't change a thing!

Play It Safe

Even though it sounds tricky, this stunt isn't too hard to set up. If you like, you can play around with adding fake wires to a battery-operated toy for the same effect. When the toy is turned on, it works and the child feels no shock from the dummy wires. However, do not for any reason add wires to electrical appliances! Don't play around with electricity or let your children see you doing so. They might try to replicate your experiment at a later date and truly shock themselves, doing great harm. So keep this activity to small batteries!

ACTIVITY 2: No Worries

Point: God doesn't want us to worry about anything.

Supplies: You'll need a Bible, paper, and pencils.

Share: When we were using the buzzer, there really wasn't anything to worry about. But sometimes we get into a scary or frustrating situation and all we can do is worry. I'd like each of us to make a list of what things worry us most in life.

Give each family member a sheet of paper and a pencil. Have everyone list things they're most likely to worry about. (Have an adult or older sibling help those who can't yet write, or allow them to draw pictures instead.) Items that cause worry might include tests at school, a job interview, sporting events, the fear of world war, confronting a friend about something, being afraid of a bully, or approaching a boss or teacher about something. Be sure to make a list yourself!

When everyone has a few items on their lists, take turns sharing. Encourage listening without making fun of others. Just because one child is afraid of the neighbor's tiny poodle, don't allow others in the family to laugh. Fears are real no matter how small they seem to others.

Share: We have quite a few things that are potential worries. Now we should look at the Bible and see what God says we should do with all these worries.

 Read Matthew 6:25-34 aloud and discuss:
- **What does this passage say about worrying?** (We shouldn't do it; God knows our needs.)
- **What should we be doing instead of worrying?** (Looking to God.)
- **How does Jesus explain why we shouldn't worry?** (God takes care of the flowers and the birds; certainly God will care for us.)

Read Philippians 4:6-7 aloud and discuss:
- **What do these verses say about worrying?** (We shouldn't worry about anything; we should tell God about our worries.)
- **What should we do instead of worrying?** (Tell God our worries; pray.)
- **What does the Bible say will happen?** (God will give us peace about the situation.)

Read Psalm 55:22 aloud and discuss:
- **What does this verse say about worrying?** (We should put our concerns before God.)
- **What do all these verses have in common?** (We shouldn't worry and we should pray about things that start to worry us.)

Share: When we pray, God sometimes changes the situation, and sometimes He doesn't. But the Bible says God will give us peace about the situation. No matter how much we worry, that won't change things. The only thing God wants us to do is pray!

Take time right now to take turns praying for each other and the items named on each list. Ask God to work in each situation, and to give all of you peace and comfort.

WRAP-UP

Gather everyone in a circle and have family members take turns answering this question: **What's one thing you've learned about God today?**

Next, tell kids you've got a new "Life Slogan" you'd like to share with them.

Life Slogan: Today's Life Slogan is this: "Don't worry. Pray and be happy." Have family members repeat the slogan two or three times to help them learn it. Then encourage them to practice saying it during the week so they can talk about it at your next family night session.

Close in Prayer: Allow time for each family member to share prayer concerns and answers to prayer. Then close your time together with prayer for each concern. Thank God for making families, especially your family! Take time to thank God for each family member, mentioning one special quality you're thankful for about that person.

Remember to record prayer requests here so you can refer to them in the future as you see God answering them.

Additional Resources:

Safe This Night by Lois Rock (ages 4–7)
We Need a Moose by Lynne Fairbridge (ages 4–7)
Bear Scare by Gayle Roper (ages 7–10)
Bruce Moose and the What-Ifs by Gary Oliver and Norman Wright (ages 4–8)

Age Adjustments

FOR YOUNGER CHILDREN, focus only on Philippians 4:6-7, to keep things more simple.

OLDER CHILDREN AND TEENS might get into a longer discussion on the fact that even though we turn things over to God, bad things still happen. For example, instead of worrying about a loved one with cancer, you might turn the situation over to God in prayer. When that loved one dies, does that mean God failed? Should you have worried after all? No. We can't change things by worrying, and even if what seems like the worst thing actually happens, we have to trust that God is in control and He knows the bigger picture. He loves us and will do what is best for each of us.

⊚ 5: Power Play

Exploring how the power of the Holy Spirit within us gives us strength

Scripture
- 2 Corinthians 4:7-9—We are pressed on every side but not crushed.
- 1 John 4:4—God's Spirit is greater than the one who is in the world.
- 1 Corinthians 6:19-20—Our bodies are temples for the Holy Spirit.

ACTIVITY OVERVIEW		
Activity	Summary	Pre-Session Prep
Activity 1: Cola Can Crush	Compare the crushing powers of nature to the pressures of the world.	You'll need a Bible, an empty soft-drink can, and kitchen tongs.
Activity 2: Air Force	Examine how to let God's Spirit work in us.	You'll need a Bible, a blow dryer or a vacuum cleaner with an air exit hose, and a Ping-Pong ball.

Main Points:

—The Holy Spirit gives us strength to withstand the pressures of the world.

—We should honor the Holy Spirit instead of blocking Him.

LIFE SLOGAN: "Greater is He that is in me than he that is in the world."

Make it your own
In the space provided below, outline the flow and add any additional ideas to guide you through the process of conducting this family night.

Prayer & Praise Items
In the space provided below, list any items you wish to pray about or give praise for during this family night session.

Journal
In the space provided below, capture a record of any fun or meaningful things which happened during this family night session.

Session Tip

We intentionally have provided more material than we would expect to be used in a single "Family Night" session. You know your family's unique interests and life circumstances best, so feel free to adapt this session to meet your family members' needs. Remember, short and simple is better than long and comprehensive.

WARM-UP

Open with Prayer: Begin by having a family member pray, asking God to help everyone in the family understand more about Him through this time. After prayer, review your last lesson by asking these questions:

- **What do you remember from our last lesson?**
- **Do you remember the Life Slogan?**
- **What was one fun thing we did during our last lesson?**
- **How has what we learned last week changed your actions in the past few days?**

Share: Today we'll be exploring how the power of the Holy Spirit gives us strength.

ACTIVITY 1: Cola Can Crush

Point: The Holy Spirit gives us strength to withstand the pressures of the world.

 Supplies: You'll need a Bible, an empty soft-drink can, and kitchen tongs.

Activity: Gather everyone in the kitchen. First, fill your sink with cold water. Then pour about an inch of water into the soft-drink can. Place the can directly on your stove burner and turn on the heat. Watch together until you see wisps of steam coming out of the can, or until you can hear the water boiling inside. Take the tongs and pick up the can. (Be sure kids stand aside to give you a clear path to the sink. No burns, please!) Over the sink, quickly flip the can over and into the water. The can must be completely upside down, with the opening of the can

Age Adjustments

FOR YOUNGER CHILDREN, the concept of the Holy Spirit within us is abstract. Try illustrating this point using a puppet. Without a hand in the puppet, the puppet is lifeless. But when you place your hand inside, the puppet "comes to life." In the same way, the Holy Spirit gives us life and strength to do things we couldn't do on our own.

FOR OLDER KIDS, have an egg-protecting contest. Give everyone the opportunity to wrap, box, or otherwise protect a raw egg. Then drop these from your roof and see how well the eggs survive. Then discuss how God has given us fragile bodies and spirits, just as the eggs are fragile. But God has also given us, as Christians, the Holy Spirit as strength for the drops and crashes of our lives.

entering the water first. The can will crush itself instantly!

Kids are likely to want to see this trick a few times, so you might want to have extra soft-drink cans on hand. Also, if the trick doesn't work on the first try, experiment with less water in the can. Be sure you're not putting the can on its side when you place it in the water.

When you're done with this fun science experiment, discuss:
- **Do you have any idea how the can crushed itself?** (Without getting too scientific, the hot air inside the can is lighter than the cold water outside the can. The weight of the heavier cold water is what crushes the can.)
- **Do you ever feel like you're that can? Like situations around you are so difficult, so heavy, that they're crushing you?**

Share: God knows all the pressures we feel each day. In fact, the Bible talks about this very feeling.

 Read 2 Corinthians 4:7-9 aloud, then ask these questions:
- **What do you think the treasure is that's in jars of clay?** (The treasure is God's forgiveness, eternal life, a relationship with God.)
- **What, or who, are the jars of clay?** (We are; humans.)
- **What's so special about jars of clay?** (Nothing!)

Share: These verses are a word picture. Paul, the writer of these verses, was comparing Christians to jars of clay. A jar of clay would break very easily. But God put His treasure of love and forgiveness into us, breakable jars. And what does the Bible say happens once God's treasure is in these human jars? (We have troubles but aren't broken or destroyed.)
- **How are we like the jars of clay, or like the aluminum can?** (We're not very strong; we're easily broken or hurt.)
- **How does having God the Holy Spirit within us change that?** (We're still weak, but God is strong and won't allow us to be crushed inside.)
- **What are things you experience each day that make you feel like you're being crushed?** (School; pressure from

friends; difficulty at work; financial concerns.)
- **How does God help you with these pressures?**

Share: God has provided Christians with the Holy Spirit as strength to withstand the pressures of the world. Even though life seems hard at times, God is with us, and within us, to give us the strength we need to stand strong against sin, temptations, and other pressures.

ACTIVITY 2: Air Force

Point: We should honor the Holy Spirit instead of blocking Him.

 Supplies: You'll need a Bible, a blow dryer or a vacuum cleaner with an air exit hose, and a Ping-Pong ball.

Activity: Hold the blow dryer or hose so it's pointing straight into the air, and turn it on. Hold a Ping-Pong ball in this air stream and let go. Watch what happens. The ball will stay balanced in the stream of air. Let your children take turns holding the blow dryer or hose and dropping the ball into the air flow. If you like, experiment with other balls, such as Nerf balls, beach balls, and so on, to see if the air stream can hold them up as well. Then put the balls away and discuss:
- **What was holding up the ball?**
- **We can't see the air, but its power to hold the ball was strong. How is this like the power of the Holy Spirit?** (We can't see the Holy Spirit, but the power of the Holy Spirit is strong.)

 Read 1 John 4:4 aloud and discuss:
- **Who is the "one who is in you" this verse is talking about?** (The Holy Spirit; God's Spirit.)

Share: Even though there was air all around the ball that would have let it fall, the air from the vacuum was strong enough to overcome the other air. God's Spirit is stronger than any other force we encounter, and God won't let us fall! Just as this verse tells us, the power within us, the Holy Spirit, is greater than any power in the world.

Now place your hand between the blower and the ball. Ask these questions:
- **Why won't the trick work anymore?** (The air is blocked; the hand keeps the full power of the air from coming out.)

• **What do you think this has to do with learning about our relationship with the Holy Spirit?**

Share: When we don't listen to the Holy Spirit, or only listen and obey when we want to, it's like we're blocking God's power from working in our lives. Like the ball, we never get anywhere. We want to allow God's Holy Spirit to live inside us and change us so we're no longer tossed or spun about by the world's ideas. Instead of blocking the Holy Spirit, we need to show honor and obedience.

• **How can we honor the Holy Spirit?** (By obeying the Bible; by being kind, loving, and patient or by demonstrating other fruits of the Spirit; with our actions.)

Share: The Bible tells us in 1 Corinthians 6:19-20 that our bodies are a temple for the Holy Spirit. Let's read that.

 Read 1 Corinthians 6:19-20 aloud, then discuss:

• **What are ways we can honor God with our bodies?** (Answers will vary depending upon the ages of your children, but might include abstaining from premarital sex, not smoking, not using drugs, exercising, eating healthful foods, getting enough rest, filling our minds with good thoughts, and so on.)

• **How do you think you're doing at honoring the temple of the Holy Spirit, your body?**

Share: Just as we wouldn't dump trash into our church, so we shouldn't dump trash into our bodies. There are many ways to honor God, and one of them is to care for our bodies.

Now might be a great time to take a family walk together, go for a bike ride, or talk about changing eating habits. Of course, if you usually end your family night with ice cream, we don't want to rain on your parade! Maybe you could try low-fat frozen yogurt tonight.

🐟 WRAP-UP

Gather everyone in a circle and have family members take turns answering this question: **What's one thing you've learned about God today?**

Next, tell kids you've got a new "Life Slogan" you'd like to share with them.

Life Slogan: Today's Life Slogan is this: "Greater is He that is in me than he that is in the world." Have family members repeat the slogan two or three times to help them learn it. Then encourage them to practice saying it during the week so they can talk about it at your next family night session.

Close in Prayer: Allow time for each family member to share prayer concerns and answers to prayer. Then close your time together with prayer for each concern. Thank God for making families, especially your family! Take time to thank God for each family member, mentioning one special quality you're thankful for about that person.

Remember to record prayer requests here so you can refer to them in the future as you see God answering them.

Additional Resources:

The King Without a Shadow by R.C. Sproul
Smokescreen Secret by Marianne Hering (ages 10–14)

6: Whistle While You Work

Exploring the problem of laziness

Scripture
• 2 Thessalonians 3:6-15—If you don't work, you don't eat.
• Proverbs 6:6-11—Learn how to work by the example of the ants.
• 1 Thessalonians 4:11-12—Hard work earns the respect of others.

ACTIVITY OVERVIEW		
Activity	Summary	Pre-Session Prep
Activity 1: Lazy Boy	Learn what it means to be a sluggard.	You'll need a Bible.
Activity 2: Insect Examples	Observe a true worker in the ant.	You'll need a video or picture books on ants, pipe cleaners, and a Bible.

Main Points:

—God has no use for sluggards.

—Be like the ant in how you approach your work.

LIFE SLOGAN: "I will work hard and not be bored. I will work for the Lord!"

Make it your own

In the space provided below, outline the flow and add any additional ideas to guide you through the process of conducting this family night.

Prayer & Praise Items

In the space provided below, list any items you wish to pray about or give praise for during this family night session.

Journal

In the space provided below, capture a record of any fun or meaningful things which happened during this family night session.

Session Tip

We intentionally have provided more material than we would expect to be used in a single "Family Night" session. You know your family's unique interests and life circumstances best, so feel free to adapt this lesson to meet your family members' needs. Remember, short and simple is better than long and comprehensive.

WARM-UP

Open with Prayer: Begin by having a family member pray, asking God to help everyone in the family understand more about Him through this time. After prayer, review your last lesson by asking these questions:

- **What do you remember from our last lesson?**
- **Do you remember the Life Slogan?**
- **What was one fun thing we did during our last lesson?**
- **How has what we learned last week changed your actions in the past few days?**

Share: Today we'll be looking at the problem of laziness.

ACTIVITY 1: Lazy Boy

Point: God has no use for sluggards.

 Supplies: Prepare for this evening by leaving several household chores undone. For example, leave the laundry unfolded, the dishes unwashed, and the trash can full. You'll also need a Bible.

Activity: Begin your time together by explaining that you and your spouse need a rest. However, there's still a lot of work that needs to be done. This means the kids will have to do it all. Assign work, requiring the children to do the uncompleted chores. Tell them to get busy while you relax.

Ignore any complaints as you and your spouse stretch out on the couch or in the recliner. Then start calling out for the kids to bring you things. "Jenny, bring me a glass of iced tea!" "Ron, I can't find the remote and don't want to bother looking for it. Will you come change the channel for me?"

Keep up your requests, as well as urging the children to hurry up and finish their chores so you can get started with family night.

After about five minutes of this, stop everything, call everyone together, and ask:

- **How do you feel about me telling you to do chores and at the same time demanding that you wait on me?**
- **Even though you don't like to be treated this way, do you ever treat others like this?**
- **What do all the following statements have in common?**

(Fill in the names of your family members as you read these.)
*"It's [name]'s turn to do the dishes. I did them yesterday."
*"Mom gave that job to [name]."
*"None of those clothes are mine. Why should I have to pick them up?"
*"I already picked up my stuff. The rest belongs to [name]."
*"[Name] got all these toys out. It wasn't me!"

Share: All of these are excuses, and they all are intended to get you out of work! You see Mom and Dad working every day at their jobs, working around the house, running errands for you, and so on. What do you think God says about work?

After children have had a chance to tell what they think, share: God warns us against being sluggards. What's a sluggard? (A dreamer; a loafer; a lazy person; an irresponsible person; someone you can't count on; someone who does what feels good for him without thinking of others.)

Share: We can find out even more about God's view of sluggards by reading the Bible.

Read 2 Thessalonians 3:6-15 aloud, then discuss:

- **What does the Bible say about doing your work?** (If you don't work, you don't eat; don't be a burden to others; a person who won't work is like an enemy.)
- **How are we supposed to treat a Christian who is lazy?** (Stay away from him or her; don't give that person your food.)
- **Why would Paul, the writer of these verses, say loving Christians should do this?** (Paul hoped that being hungry, lonely, and ashamed would teach people that they need to work and be productive.)

Share: When Paul wrote this letter, many Christians believed Jesus would be returning to take them to heaven any day. So they thought they could just sit around and wait. They didn't think they needed to do any work. Instead, they mooched off other people who were working. God wanted Christians to know this is wrong. Being ready for Christ to return doesn't mean sitting around all the time. Instead, it means that we should obey God and have our hearts ready all the time. And while we are waiting, there is still plenty of work to do!

Make a family agreement that for the next week you'll live by the rule of this passage, "If you don't work, you don't eat." Clarify what this means. For example, if your homework or chores aren't done before the appropriate meal, you can't eat. At the end of the week, ask each person to evaluate how much more quickly they did their work, knowing the consequences of putting it off.

Then take time to join together and get those chores completed as a team. Put on some happy music and whistle while you work!

Age Adjustments

This lesson might be too difficult for VERY YOUNG CHILDREN to do. Instead, help them list their chores or responsibilities. Then together determine when these chores are to be done, and the consequences of not doing them. For example, toys must be picked up by 3 P.M. or no watching Barney. Or teeth must be brushed before 7 P.M. or there won't be a bedtime story. Discuss 2 Thessalonians 3:10 and why it's important for each person to take care of his or her work. What would happen if no one did their jobs? What would happen if Mom decided to stop cooking meals? What if Dad decided to stop doing the laundry? Agree to work together as a family with a happy attitude, with each person doing his or her jobs in a timely manner.

ACTIVITY 2: Insect Examples

Point: Be like the ant in how you approach your work.

Supplies: You'll need a video about ants (check your local library). If a video isn't available, look for picture books on ants or articles in an encyclopedia. You'll also need a Bible.

Activity: Turn on the video about ants and watch it together. As you watch, comment on the hard work ants do, how they can lift more than their own weight, and so on.

After the video, share: No one tells the ants what to do.

No one inspects their work. But still, each one does his work, no matter how hard it is, without stopping. They plan ahead, store food, and keep busy. You might be surprised to learn that the Bible talks about ants!

Activity: Give each child pipe cleaners to make ants while you continue the lesson.

Read Proverbs 6:6-11 aloud and discuss:
- **What can we learn from the ants after watching the video and reading what the Bible says about them?** (We would be wise to follow the example of the ants; if we are lazy too much, we won't have food.)
- **Do you think you're a better worker than an insect? Why or why not?**
- **How can each of us improve our attitudes and actions in the area of work?**

Share: The Bible tells us more about why work is so important to God.

Read 1 Thessalonians 4:11-12, then ask:
- **What's the importance of work?** (To win the respect of people who aren't Christians; so we won't have to depend on others for our food and other needs.)
- **How does working hard help others respect us?** (They don't resent our sitting around while they do all the hard work; they see we don't expect others to cater to our desires; others can see how much we appreciate them by how hard we work to help them.)
- **How does working hard help us to be independent?** (We don't have to rely on friends, family, the government, or others to feed and clothe us; we know how much work has to be done to gain the necessities of life, so we don't want to rob others of what they've worked hard to earn.)

Share: We can be more effective in showing others our love for God by our attitudes and actions regarding work. We often talk about being models or examples for others in the areas of love and forgiveness, but we should also be models or examples in the way we pitch in and get a job done. No matter how small or big the job is, we should have the attitude of "I'm doing this job for God!" That can help us do our best and realize that even if other people don't appreciate what we do, God does!

Age Adjustments

FOR YOUNGER CHILDREN, add to this lesson by singing "The Ants Come Marching" as you march in a line around your house. The tune is "When Johnny Comes Marching Home Again." Even if you don't know the tune, you can march around and chant the words.

> The ants come marching one by one,
> Hurrah, hurrah.
> The ants come marching one by one,
> Hurrah, hurrah.
> The ants come marching one by one,
> The little one stops to suck his thumb.
> And they all go marching
> Down,
> To the ground,
> To get out,
> Of the rain.
> Boom, boom, boom!

Continue with the second verse, "The ants come marching two by two," and have "the little one stop" to do something that rhymes with that number. (Two—stops to tie his shoe; Three—stops to rub his knee; and so on.) Make as many silly rhymes as you can!

FOR OLDER CHILDREN AND TEENAGERS, add to this lesson by having each family member, including you, list all their work. Include homework, school, going to work, washing dishes, mending, yard work, packing lunches, driving others to school or events, and so on. Then compare lists. Is each person doing his fair share? Is any one person mooching off the work of others? (Be prepared to find it might even be you who's doing less than others!) How can the lists be changed so that each person is doing a fair amount? Is everyone willing to make these adjustments? What would God consider to be the right thing to do?

 WRAP-UP

Gather everyone in a circle and have family members take turns answering this question: **What's one thing you've learned about God today?**

Next, tell kids you've got a new "Life Slogan" you'd like to share with them.

Life Slogan: Today's Life Slogan is this: "I will work hard and not be bored. I will work for the Lord!" Have family members repeat the slogan two or three times to help them learn it. Then encourage them to practice saying it during the week so they can talk about it at your next family night session.

Close in Prayer: Allow time for each family member to share prayer concerns and answers to prayer. Then close your time together with prayer for each concern. Thank God for making families, especially your family! Take time to thank God for each family member, mentioning one special quality you're thankful for about that person.

Remember to record prayer requests here so you can refer to them in the future as you see God answering them.

Additional Resources:

Hero for a Season by Nancy Simpson Levene (ages 8–12)
Rattlebang Helps by Mark McCord (ages 2–4)
Fab Day Video #10—Happy Helpers (ages 3–8)

☉ 7: A Prayer a Day

Exploring why it's important to pray, and what keeps us from prayer

Scripture
- Luke 10:38-42—The story of Mary and Martha.
- Matthew 5:23-24—Reconcile with others before praying.
- 1 Peter 3:7—Treatment of others affects our prayers.

ACTIVITY OVERVIEW		
Activity	**Summary**	**Pre-Session Prep**
Activity 1: Can You Hear Me?	Compare prayer with a telephone line.	You'll need a Bible, two paper cups, two paper clips, and fishing line.
Activity 2: Constant Contact	Discover the importance of prayer in our daily lives.	You'll need blindfolds.

Main Points:

—Sin and busyness can interfere with our prayers.

—We must be in constant contact with God.

LIFE SLOGAN: "Pray throughout the day to help you know God's way!"

Make it your own

In the space provided below, outline the flow and add any additional ideas to guide you through the process of conducting this family night.

Prayer & Praise Items

In the space provided below, list any items you wish to pray about or give praise for during this family night session.

Journal

In the space provided below, capture a record of any fun or meaningful things which happened during this family night session.

Session Tip

We intentionally have provided more material than we would expect to be used in a single "Family Night" session. You know your family's unique interests and life circumstances best, so feel free to adapt this lesson to meet your family members' needs. Remember, short and simple is better than long and comprehensive.

WARM-UP

Open with Prayer: Begin by having a family member pray, asking God to help everyone in the family understand more about Him through this time. After prayer, review your last lesson by asking these questions:

- **What do you remember from our last lesson?**
- **Do you remember the Life Slogan?**
- **What was one fun thing we did during our last lesson?**
- **How has what we learned last week changed your actions in the past few days?**

Share: During this family night, we'll be learning more about prayer.

ACTIVITY 1: Can You Hear Me?

Point: Sin and busyness can interfere with our prayers.

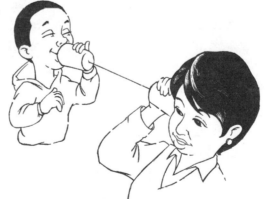

Supplies: You'll need a Bible, two paper cups, two paper clips, and a long length of fishing line, or paper megaphones and socks.

Activity: Have your children help you make a simple telephone system. Poke a small hole in the bottom of each paper cup. String the fishing line through the hole, from the outside bottom of the cup to the inside. On the inside, tie the string to a paper clip so that when it's gently pulled upon, the paper clip keeps the string attached to the cup. Repeat with the other cup, paper clip, and end of the fishing line.

Lay the line across chairs, under couches, and around other obstacles. Give one end to two of your children (or one child and yourself, if you only have one child), and have them attempt to talk and listen to each other through the cups. If you have other children, let them try as well. It doesn't work!

Then try "clearing" the line by making it straight and taut. Try talking and listen to each other again. This time it should work. (Note: If you don't have strings which will work well, change the activity to using paper megaphones. With a sock stuffed inside they don't work. Without the sock they do.) After everyone's had a chance to talk, put the telephone aside and discuss:

- **What was the difference between the two tries with the phone system?**
- **How is talking to God sometimes like this situation?** (Sometimes other things get in the way of our prayers; we can get "interference" in our conversations with God just like we had interference on our phone line.)
- **What things interfere with your talking to or praying to God?**

Share: The Bible mentions two things that often get in the way of our talking to God. We can learn about the first in Luke 10:38-42.

Read the story of sisters Mary and Martha in Luke 10:38-42 aloud, then discuss:

- **What was important to Martha?** (Getting dinner ready; cleaning the house; doing chores.)
- **What was important to Mary?** (Listening to Jesus.)
- **After listening to this story, what do you think is one thing that can get in the way of our prayers?** (Being too busy; forgetting to take time to pray; forgetting that prayer is more important than doing other things.)

Share: Remember the phone line? When the phone line was wound around other things, it wouldn't work. When our lives are wound up in too many activities and interests, these interfere with our prayers. Psalm 46:10 reminds us to "Be still, and know that I am God." That means that even though it's important to do our work, it's also important to take time out for talking to God. Now let's find out what the other thing is that can interfere with our prayers.

Read Matthew 5:23-24 and 1 Peter 3:7 aloud, then discuss:

- **What do these verses suggest will get in the way of our prayers?** (Not getting along with others; having an argu-

ment or bad feelings between you and others; sin.)
- **Why do you think sin gets in the way of prayers?** (We're busy thinking about our anger or how to hurt others instead of thinking about our love for God; God won't be forgiving to us if we're not forgiving to others.)

Share: Even if the other person is in the wrong, the Bible tells us to resolve our differences and extend love to others. Then we'll be able to pray to God without anything getting in the way.

Take time now to evaluate how to make more time for prayer, individually or as a family. Also ask each person to consider how sin might be interfering with his or her prayers. Now's a great time to ask for forgiveness!

ACTIVITY 2: Constant Contact

Point: We must be in constant contact with God.

Supplies: You'll need blindfolds.

Activity: Using the furniture in your home, create a mazelike obstacle course. Then blindfold one of your children and have that one ask another child (or yourself) to guide him or her through the course by voice commands. When you stop talking, the child should stop walking. (Pause every now and then.)

Do this again with your other children until each person (including you) has had a chance to go through the course. To make it more difficult, change the course after each round, or change it after the person is blindfolded. That way they won't be able to plan their steps ahead of time.

After everyone has had a turn, ask:
- **What made it easy or hard for you to go through the maze?**
- **Can you think of how this game might relate to prayer?**

Share: In order to get though this maze, you had to listen to the voice of someone who could see the maze. In order to get through the maze of life, or to understand what God wants you to do each day, you need to listen to what God is telling you. You need to be in constant communication with God. The maze is like God's plan for your life. You can't see it all, but God can. If you stop talking to God and listening for His guidance, you won't know where to go next. You'll start to feel lost because you won't know what to do or where to turn. Prayer

is a way to keep in constant contact with God.

Take time right now to pray for God's guidance for your whole family. If there are upcoming decisions to be made, pray for clear direction from God in these decisions. Then take time to listen.

WRAP-UP

Gather everyone in a circle and have family members take turns answering this question: **What's one thing you've learned about God today?**

Next, tell kids you've got a new "Life Slogan" you'd like to share with them.

Life Slogan: Today's Life Slogan is this: "Pray throughout the day to help you know God's way!" Have family members repeat the slogan two or three times to help them learn it. Then encourage them to practice saying it during the week so they can talk about it at your next family night session.

Close in Prayer: Allow time for each family member to share prayer concerns and answers to prayer. Then close your time together with prayer for each concern. Thank God for making families, especially your family! Take time to thank God for each family member, mentioning one special quality you're thankful for about that person.

Remember to record prayer requests here so you can refer to them in the future as you see God answering them.

Additional Resources:

What Happens When Children Pray by Evelyn Christenson (ages 4–7)
Mint Cookie Miracles by Nancy Simpson Levene (ages 7–10)
I Can Talk to God by Christine Tangvald (ages 1–3)
A First Look at Prayer by Lois Rock (ages 4–7)

@ 8: It's a Great Day!

Exploring the joy we can experience being alive in the Lord

Scripture
- Psalm 118:24—Let us rejoice each day.
- Lamentations 3:22-23—God's mercies are new each day.
- Proverbs 16:9—God determines our steps.

ACTIVITY OVERVIEW		
Activity	Summary	Pre-Session Prep
Activity 1: Up, Up, and Away!	Compare a fun experiment to our daily attitudes toward life.	You'll need a small plastic bottle, a cork to fit the bottle's opening, water, vinegar, paper towels, baking soda, and a Bible.
Activity 2: A Daily Gift	Learn of God's plan and purpose for our lives.	You'll need a Bible.

Main Points:

—For Christians, each day should be faced with joy.

—Every day, good or bad, is a gift from God.

LIFE SLOGAN: "View each day as God's gift, and it will give your heart a lift!"

Make it your own
In the space provided below, outline the flow and add any additional ideas to guide you through the process of conducting this family night.

Prayer & Praise Items
In the space provided below, list any items you wish to pray about or give praise for during this family night session.

Journal
In the space provided below, capture a record of any fun or meaningful things which happened during this family night session.

Session Tip

We intentionally have provided more material than we would expect to be used in a single "Family Night" session. You know your family's unique interests and life circumstances best, so feel free to adapt this lesson to meet your family members' needs. Remember, short and simple is better than long and comprehensive.

WARM-UP

Open with Prayer: Begin by having a family member pray, asking God to help everyone in the family understand more about Him through this time. After prayer, review your last lesson by asking these questions:

- **What do you remember from our last lesson?**
- **Do you remember the Life Slogan?**
- **What was one fun thing we did during our last lesson?**
- **How has what we learned last week changed your actions in the past few days?**

Share: Today we're going to find out why each day is special and a reason to celebrate.

ACTIVITY 1: Up, Up, and Away!

Point: For Christians, each day should be faced with joy.

Supplies: You'll need a small plastic bottle (such as a 16-ounce soft-drink bottle), a cork to fit the bottle's opening, water, vinegar, paper towels, baking soda, and a Bible. For safety reasons, please don't use glass bottles for this activity.

Activity: Give each person in your family the opportunity to complete this sentence: **For Christians, each day should be _____ .**

No answer is wrong. This will just give each person a chance to express his or her thoughts.

After everyone has shared, **read** Psalm 118:24 aloud, then ask:
- **What does the Bible say we should do each day?** (Rejoice and be glad.)

• **Why do you think God wants us to rejoice and be glad?**
• **What has God done that gives us reason to rejoice?** (Sent Christ to die for our sins; given us food; provided our family; and so on.)

Share: I know a fun experiment we can do that will help us learn more about facing each day with joy.

Age Adjustments

FOR ALL AGES, add to this activity by having a time of trying new things! Prepare or purchase unusual fruits or vegetables to try, or go to a new restaurant (an ethnic restaurant would be best) and have everyone order a food they've never tried. Play a new game, learn a new word or fact, and so on. Get everyone into the excitement of the newness of life, over and over again!

Go outside for this experiment. Take the bottle and pour about a half cup of water and a half cup of vinegar into it. Then take a square of paper towel, about four by four inches, and place two teaspoons of baking soda on the center of it. Roll the paper towel and twist the ends to make a little capsule of baking soda. Then drop this capsule into the bottle, quickly place the cork over the opening, and stand back to see what happens!

Because carbon dioxide forms in the bottle, the pressure of the gas will eventually pop the cork off the bottle. Children love this experiment and will most likely want to try it again and again. You can try varying the amounts of water, vinegar, and baking soda to see how high or far you can get the cork to pop.

When you're done with the experiment, clean up the supplies and return to your normal meeting area. Discuss this question:

• **What do you think this experiment has to do with facing each day with joy?** (The explosion is like fireworks; it's a lot of fun; it's exciting.)

Share: Each day, God launches us, like the cork, into the world to do His work. We can start each day with a bang and an attitude of joy knowing that God has made this new day for us to enjoy!

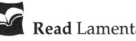 **Read** Lamentations 3:22-23 aloud, then ask this question:

• **What does this verse say about each new day?** (God's compassions, or mercies, are new every morning; God is faithful; because of God's great love, we can have strength to face each day.)

Share: Every day God has something new for us. This might be a new person to meet, something new to learn, or a new place to go. It might

be a small thing, like a new bird singing or a new food to try, or something big, like moving to a new home, new school, or new job. These are reasons to have joy. Also, God's love and mercy are new each day. God doesn't hold the sins of yesterday in front of us. Instead, we face each day afresh. We have much to be thankful for—and much to look forward to. That's why Christians can face each day with joy!

ACTIVITY 2: A Daily Gift

Point: Every day, good or bad, is a gift from God.

Supplies: You'll need a Bible.

Share: Another thing we can learn from our experiment has to do with the cork. When the cork popped off the bottle, it flew this way and that. We could never tell where it would end up. But God's plan for us isn't like that. Let's read Proverbs 16:9 to see how we're different from the cork.

Read Proverbs 16:9 aloud, then discuss:
- **What does this verse tell us?** (Even if we plan our steps, God is the one who determines where we'll go.)
- **How is this different from the cork?** (The cork lands anywhere, but God has a plan for our path or where we'll "land.")
- **Have you ever felt like a cork, flying out of control? If so, tell about that time.**
- **Do you feel like God's in control of your path even on "bad" days? Why or why not?**

Share: Sometimes we have a bad day, or even a bad week. It seems like everything goes wrong for us. Those days are difficult to face with joy. But those days are still gifts from God. We might not realize now what we're learning from hard times, but God can use bad days and good days to help us grow and learn more about Him.

Have each family member think of a time when they had a bad day or a hard week but it turned out for something good. For example, a difficult week of studying turned into the reward of a good grade. Or the death of a loved one helped several people to become Christians.

Give each person the opportunity to share.

Share: Even during bad days or hard times, God is with us and helping us. Let me read something to you.

Footprints in the Sand

One night I had a dream. I was walking along the beach with the Lord, and across the skies flashed scenes from my life. In each scene I noticed two sets of footprints in the sand. One was mine, and one was the Lord's.

When the last scene of my life appeared before me, I looked back at the footprints in the sand, and, to my surprise, I noticed that many times along the path of my life there was only one set of footprints. And I noticed that it was at the lowest and saddest times in my life. I asked the Lord about it.

"Lord, You said that once I decided to follow You, You would walk with me all the way. But I noticed that during the most troublesome times in my life there is only one set of footprints. I don't understand why You left my side when I needed You the most."

The Lord said, "My precious child, I never left you during your time of trial. Where you see only one set of footprints, I was carrying you."

- **Have you ever had days when you felt like God was carrying you? If so, share that with us.**
- **How can you face times like this with an attitude of joy?**

Share: God knows what He has ahead for us, and knows what experiences we'll need to have to prepare for those times. Even difficult times can be a gift if we consider that God is helping us to grow.

Challenge family members to consider each day as a gift from God, no matter what the day holds. To help reinforce this, hide small gifts for family members around your home during the next week. These might be a magazine hidden under a pillow, a small box of chocolates tucked into the bathroom cabinet, a flower waiting in the refrigerator, or simply notes of encouragement left about for others to find. Family members might enjoy joining you in leaving tiny gifts for each other as well. Use this as a fun way to remind each other to look at each day as a gift from God. You never know where or when something great will turn up!

WRAP-UP

Gather everyone in a circle and have family members take turns answering this question: **What's one thing you've learned about God today?**

Next, tell kids you've got a new "Life Slogan" you'd like to share with them.

Life Slogan: Today's Life Slogan is this: "View each day as God's gift, and it will give your heart a lift!" Have family members repeat the slogan two or three times to help them learn it. Then encourage them to practice saying it during the week so they can talk about it at your next family night session.

Close in Prayer: Allow time for each family member to share prayer concerns and answers to prayer. Then close your time together with prayer for each concern. Thank God for making families, especially your family! Take time to thank God for each family member, mentioning one special quality you're thankful for about that person.

Remember to record prayer requests here so you can refer to them in the future as you see God answering them.

Additional Resources:

The Day Momma Played by Ingrid Lawrenz (ages 4–7)
Tales of the Restoration by David & Karen Mains
Sad News, Glad News by Lois Rock (ages 4–7)

Age Adjustments

This activity is too abstract for YOUNGER CHILDREN. Instead, wrap several small gifts in pretty wrapping paper, complete with bows. Consider wrapping a box with a small candy for each child, a box with a quarter for each child, a box with a coupon good for you telling a story to each child, and so on.

Place the wrapped boxes before your small children. Give them the opportunity to shake each box, then guess what might be inside. Then let the children open the gifts and share the treasures they find. Compare these gifts to the prospect of each new day. We don't know what's ahead each day, but we know it's something from God. That can help us look forward to each day.

@ 9: God's Garden

Exploring spiritual growth

Scripture
- 1 Peter 2:2—Spiritual milk helps us grow.
- Ephesians 4:14-15—Deceit keeps us from growing.
- Hebrews 5:11-14—Not learning and applying keeps us from growing.

ACTIVITY OVERVIEW		
Activity	Summary	Pre-Session Prep
Activity 1: My, You've Grown!	Compare measurements of physical and mental growth to measurements of spiritual growth.	You'll need family photograph albums showing your children at different ages (or family videos); a tape measure; a bathroom scale; and a Bible.
Activity 2: Strong Sprouts	Identify hindrances to our growth.	You'll need plants and a Bible.

Main Points:

—Just as we grow physically and mentally, we need to grow spiritually.

—We should avoid things that keep us from growing.

LIFE SLOGAN: "Know more to grow more."

Make it your own

In the space provided below, outline the flow and add any additional ideas to guide you through the process of conducting this family night.

Prayer & Praise Items

In the space provided below, list any items you wish to pray about or give praise for during this family night session.

Journal

In the space provided below, capture a record of any fun or meaningful things which happened during this family night session.

Session Tip

We intentionally have provided more material than we would expect to be used in a single "Family Night" session. You know your family's unique interests and life circumstances best, so feel free to adapt this session to meet your family members' needs. Remember, short and simple is better than long and comprehensive.

WARM-UP

Open with Prayer: Begin by having a family member pray, asking God to help everyone in the family understand more about Him through this time. After prayer, review your last lesson by asking these questions:

- **What do you remember from our last lesson?**
- **Do you remember the Life Slogan?**
- **What was one fun thing we did during our last lesson?**
- **How has what we learned last week changed your actions in the past few days?**

Share: Today we'll be learning about what it means to grow spiritually.

ACTIVITY 1: My, You've Grown!

Point: Just as we grow physically and mentally, we need to grow spiritually.

 Supplies: You'll need family photograph albums showing your children at different ages (or family videos); a tape measure; a bathroom scale; and a Bible.

Activity: Gather family members around for a fun time of looking through family photo albums or watching family videos. As you look together, comment on the growth of your children, how they've changed physically, what they've learned to do over the years, and so on.

When the last picture has been viewed, pull out your tape

measure and see how tall each person is. If you like, mark this on a wall or door frame. Then weigh each person (no fair skipping this, Mom and Dad!) and note how much family members weigh. If you still remember (or can look up the information), share with your children their lengths and weights at birth. Compare these to their current measurements. How much growth has taken place in each person?

Then gather to discuss:

- **What are things you can do now that you couldn't do a year ago?** (Read; ride a bike; do division; drive a car; and so on.)
- **What had to happen for you to be able to do these things?** (Grow; become older; become more mature.)
- **What are other ways you've changed in the past year?** (Interests might have changed; friends might have changed; job skills might be different; and so on.)
- **We know we need to grow, but what makes us grow?** (Food; exercise; experiences; love; school.)
- **What are things we can make grow faster?** (Muscles; knowledge; skills; speech.)
- **What are things we can't make grow faster?** (Height; our age.)

Share: God made us to grow physically and mentally, and we've been looking at how we've done these things over the years. But God also wants us to grow spiritually.

 Read 1 Peter 2:2 aloud, then ask these questions:

- **What does it mean to crave something?** (To want it badly; to think you can't live without it.)
- **What is spiritual milk?** (Anything from God that causes us to grow spiritually; studying the Bible; learning from other Christians.)
- **Why do we need this milk?** (So we'll grow spiritually; so we'll grow in our salvation; so we'll grow closer to God; so we'll be more like Christ.)
- **Why do you think God wants us to grow in this way?** (So we'll be more like Jesus; so we'll be strong against sin; so we can enjoy life; so we can help others learn about God.)

Age Adjustments

FOR OLDER CHILDREN, continue this discussion by reading 2 Peter 1:5-11. How can we add these qualities to our lives? How do these qualities make us effective and productive Christians? How does lacking these qualities make us nearsighted or blind? What can we do right now to help us have attitudes of eagerness toward spiritual growth?

Share: We can feed our bodies and minds to help them grow, and we can also feed our spirits so they will grow. We do this by reading our Bibles, learning at church, talking with other Christians, praying, and going through hard times. Even our family nights are a way to help us grow spiritually.

ACTIVITY 2: Strong Sprouts

Point: We should avoid things that keep us from growing.

 Supplies: You'll need seeds, plants (such as house plants at various stages of growth, or a garden or nursery to tour), and a Bible.

Share: Now we know what helps us grow spiritually, but sometimes things get in the way of our growth. To help us understand this, I've brought us a few plants to look at.

Bring out a few of your house plants, wander through your vegetable or flower garden, or take a tour of a plant nursery. After you've explored the plant life of God's world, discuss:

- **These plants grow from little seeds or cuttings from other plants. They go from being tiny and weak to being strong, healthy, beautiful, and fruitful. What would keep these plants from growing?** (No water; no soil; no light; too much water; too much light.)
- **What things keep us from growing physically?** (Eating too much junk food; not exercising; not getting the right nutrients.)
- **What could keep us from growing mentally?** (Not going to school; not learning to read; not challenging our minds to tackle new problems.)
- **What do you think keeps us from growing spiritually?** (Not reading the Bible; not learning at church; avoiding situations that would help us grow.)

Share: Let's find out what the Bible says about things that hinder our spiritual growth.

Read Ephesians 4:14-15 aloud, then discuss:
- **According to this passage, what are things that can keep us**

from growing from spiritual babies into mature
Christians? (Listening to wrong teaching; following men or
women who deceive us.)

- **What are examples of these?** (Your family will have a
variety of answers depending on their ages, but possible
answers could include following "friends" who try to get
them to lie, steal, use drugs or participate in other sins;
getting involved with cults or religions that don't believe
in the Bible or that add to the Bible; or focusing on tiny,
unimportant bits of theology and philosophy instead of
obeying God's commands to love Him and others.)

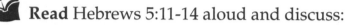 Read Hebrews 5:11-14 aloud and discuss:

- **According to this passage, what keeps us from growing?**
(Being slow to learn; eating only milk and not solid food.)
- **What are examples of this happening?** (Someone who goes
to church but never listens to or applies the teaching; someone who reads the Bible occasionally but doesn't do what
the Bible says; someone who has the attitude that he doesn't
need to learn anything.)
- **What does this passage say is an example of someone who
has grown spiritually?** (He teaches others about God; she
can tell good from evil.)
- **How can we avoid these hindrances to spiritual growth?**
(Focus on what helps us to grow; have an attitude of wanting
to grow; identify things that keep us from growing, and
when we see them in our lives or around us, get away!)

**Share: There are elements our bodies, plants, and other living things
need and don't need in order to grow. In the same way, there are
things we need to do, and things we need to avoid, in order to grow
spiritually. Let's move on from milk and eat solid foods!**

WRAP-UP
Gather everyone in a circle and have family members take
turns answering this question: **What's one thing you've learned
about God today?**

Next, tell kids you've got a new "Life Slogan" you'd like to share
with them.

Life Slogan: Today's Life Slogan is this: "Know more to grow more."
Have family members repeat the slogan two or three times to help

Age Adjustments

YOUNGER CHILDREN might not understand the hindrances to spiritual growth. Instead, focus on what helps us to grow. Pull out a "food pyramid" showing what foods we need to eat to grow (many cereal boxes display these, or check a health-food store). Together plan a day's menu around this pyramid, choosing foods in the appropriate portions. Then plan a spiritual menu, choosing activities for a day that will help you grow spiritually, such as a short Scripture reading or the sharing of a Bible story, and a time of prayer together. Then carry out both of these menus.

OLDER CHILDREN might learn more about growth through a trip to the library. Research Asian cultures that once bound the feet of wealthy baby girls to keep their feet from growing. Why did they do this, and what was the result? Even though this practice was meant to show status, what were other results of it? What are things that bind us and keep us from growing closer to God? How can we get rid of these bindings?

them learn it. Then encourage them to practice saying it during the week so they can talk about it at your next family night session.

Close in Prayer: Allow time for each family member to share prayer concerns and answers to prayer. Then close your time together with prayer for each concern. Thank God for making families, especially your family! Take time to thank God for each family member, mentioning one special quality you're thankful for about that person.

Remember to record prayer requests here so you can refer to them in the future as you see God answering them.

Additional Resources:

A First Look at the Bible by Lois Rock (ages 4–7)
Adam Raccoon and the Flying Machine by Glen Keane (ages 4–7)
Caution: Dangerous Devotions! by Jackie Perseghetti (ages 8–12)
Devotions for the Sandbox Set by Jane Morton (ages 2–5)
Discover the Bible by Lois Rock (ages 4–7)
Discovery Bible Devotions by Carla Williams (ages 4–7)
How the Bible Came to Us by Meryl Doney (ages 8–12)

☯ 10: A Strong Finish

Exploring how to finish strong even when the task is difficult

Scripture
• Genesis 6:5-22—Noah builds the ark.
• Philippians 3:10-14—Press on toward the goal of being like Christ.

ACTIVITY OVERVIEW		
Activity	Summary	Pre-Session Prep
Activity 1: Big Boat, Big Job	Compare tasks we have to the task Noah had of building the ark.	You'll need a jigsaw puzzle and a Bible.
Activity 2: Family Flight Plan	Create plans to help family members reach various goals.	You'll need the portion of a flight map on page 86, paper and pencils, and a Bible.

Main Points:

—Commitment and hard work are needed to finish strong.

—Planning helps us finish strong.

LIFE SLOGAN: "Do your best all along, and you'll be sure to finish strong!"

Make it your own

In the space provided below, outline the flow and add any additional ideas to guide you through the process of conducting this family night.

Prayer & Praise Items

In the space provided below, list any items you wish to pray about or give praise for during this family night session.

Journal

In the space provided below, capture a record of any fun or meaningful things which happened during this family night session.

Session Tip

We intentionally have provided more material than we would expect to be used in a single "Family Night" session. You know your family's unique interests and life circumstances best, so feel free to adapt this lesson to meet your family members' needs. Remember, short and simple is better than long and comprehensive.

WARM-UP

Open with Prayer: Begin by having a family member pray, asking God to help everyone in the family understand more about Him through this time. After prayer, review your last lesson by asking these questions:

- **What do you remember from our last lesson?**
- **Do you remember the Life Slogan?**
- **What was one fun thing we did during our last lesson?**
- **How has what we learned last week changed your actions in the past few days?**

Share: During our time today we'll be discovering how to finish a job, even when it seems too hard.

ACTIVITY 1: Big Boat, Big Job

Point: Commitment and hard work are needed to finish strong.

 Supplies: You'll need a jigsaw puzzle and a Bible. Be sure to choose a puzzle with a difficulty level appropriate for your children's ages. Also consider that it's important to the lesson that you complete the whole puzzle during this family time, so you won't want a 5,000-piece puzzle, no matter how advanced your children are! If there is a wide spread of ages in your family, you might consider using a simple puzzle for the younger children to complete while the older children work together on a harder puzzle.

Activity: Before your family time, place a jigsaw puzzle on a large table with the picture side of the pieces facing down.

Gather family members around the puzzle and spend time working together on completing it. Don't allow anyone to flip over the pieces and use the picture to help them figure out the puzzle. The added challenge here is that the picture isn't available for viewing. Most importantly, don't give up! Since the point of this lesson is to finish strong, finishing the puzzle is important.

As you work, talk about these questions together:
- **When were you ever given a job that seemed too hard for you to do? What happened?**
- **What situations make you feel like giving up? Think about school, relationships, jobs, community activities, sports, and so on.**
- **How do you feel when you do give up on a project?**
- **Before you begin a project, do you think about whether or not you'll be able to finish it? Explain your answer.**
- **How do you feel about others who don't finish something they've started?**

After your puzzle is completed and you've talked about these questions, read the story of Noah in Genesis 6:5-22.

Share: This boat was to be 450 feet long, 75 feet wide, and 45 feet high. It would hold about 43,000 tons!

To help family members understand the magnitude of this task, go outside and measure off the distance of the base of the ark (450 feet by 75 feet). You may have to go to a park to find enough area for these measurements. Then return to your meeting area and discuss:
- **When I gave you the puzzle to put together, how did you feel about doing it? Did you think it would be too hard? too easy?**
- **Now that the puzzle's done, how do you feel about the job of putting it together?**
- **When God told Noah to build the ark, how do you think Noah must have felt?**
- **Consider that Noah was around 500 years old when God told him to build this huge boat. And it took around 100 years to build it. Then Noah still had to get all the animals on board and get onto the boat with them for a long time. How would you feel if all this happened to you?**
- **What do you think enabled Noah to do this huge job? (We**

don't know for sure, but we can guess that he knew it was what God wanted. Some people think God made the animals come to the ark so Noah wouldn't have to find them.)

- **What things do you think were hard for Noah in building the ark?** (Again, the Bible doesn't tell us any of this information, but we can imagine it was difficult to find all the supplies, other people might have made fun of Noah, and it might have been hard to work without a lot of help.)
- **When you consider the things you think are hard, and compare them to the job Noah had to do, how does it make you feel about your tasks?**
- **What do you think we can learn from Noah?** (To work hard; to obey God; to keep working even if a job takes a long time; don't give up!)

Share: Noah trusted that God wouldn't give him a job that was more than he could handle. And because of this, Noah committed himself to the job at hand. He was willing to work hard. Commitment and hard work are both important to finishing strong.

Age Adjustments

FOR OLDER CHILDREN, read 2 Timothy 2:3-7 together and discuss the examples Paul gave. What difficulties or hardships does a soldier encounter? an athlete? a farmer? What do these people do during hard times? What's the goal for them? How does their goal help them through hard times? How can we learn from their examples?

If you like, visit a military base or police academy, an athletic training center, or a farm. Arrange for a tour to see how people must work hard to reach their goals. Ask about the difficulties they encounter. Ask about the rewards they receive as well. After the tour, determine actions and attitudes you all can incorporate into your own lives to help you face hard tasks or hard times differently.

ACTIVITY 2: Family Flight Plan

Point: Planning helps us finish strong.

Supplies: You'll need the portion of a flight map on page 86, paper and pencils, and a Bible.

Share: One thing that helps when you have a big job ahead of you is to plan your course.
Bring out the flight map on page 86 and show it to your family.

Share: This is a small section of a much larger map, but it gives you an idea of what a flight map looks like. Before a pilot leaves one airport to fly to another one, he or she has to file a flight plan that shows the course of flight the pilot plans to take. This shows the air authorities that the pilot knows where he or she is going.

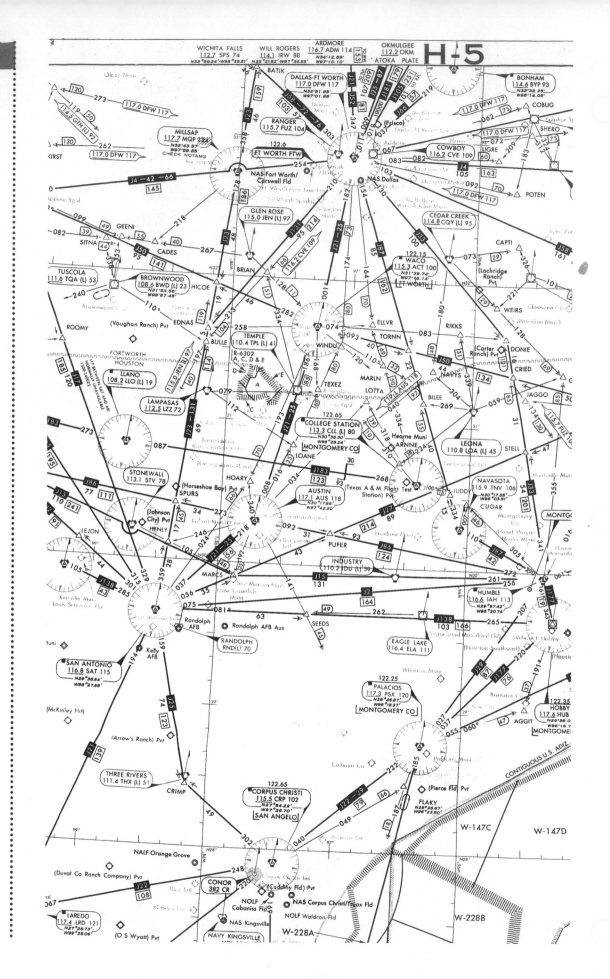

Use the map as if you were pilots. Plan flights from San Antonio International to Dallas/Fort Worth. Or chart a course from Waco to Corpus Christi. How many possible flight plans can you count just for this small section of the world?

Discuss:

- **What does the pilot need to know before leaving the airport?** (Where he or she is going; weather conditions; how to work the aircraft; storms in the way; and so on.)
- **Why does it help for others to know this flight plan?** (So people will know where to begin looking if the pilot gets lost; if the pilot starts to go the wrong way, controllers will be able to direct the pilot back onto the right path; it helps plan other flights so there won't be crashes in the air.)
- **What's the pilot's goal?** (To safely arrive at his or her destination.)
- **What are goals you have?**

Goals your family members share may be short-range or simple goals, such as passing an upcoming test, surviving the planning of a child's birthday party, or getting to work on time the next day. Or family members might express goals that will take longer to achieve, such as finishing college, getting an advancement at work, or learning to read. Encourage everyone to think of several different goals they have. Have each person write his or her goals on a sheet of paper. (Help younger children with this.)

Share: The Bible tells us about one goal we should all have in addition to our personal goals.

Read Philippians 3:10-14, then discuss:

- **What goal was Paul, the writer of these verses, talking about?** (Becoming a mature Christian; Paul wanted to become more like Christ.)
- **What's Paul's plan for getting to his goal?** (Press on; forget the past and look to the future; strain toward winning the prize of reaching his goal.)
- **How was Paul similar to a pilot?** (He knew what the goal was and was working toward getting there.)

Share: None of us would want to be on an airplane and suddenly hear the pilot say, "I give up. This is too hard and I'm not flying this plane anymore!" But since the pilot has a plan of how to get to the destination, we don't worry about getting there. In the same way, if

we have a plan of how to reach our goals, we're more likely to get there.

Return to your written goals. Ask each person to think of two or more steps they might follow as a "flight plan" to reaching this goal. For example, if the goal is to complete a science project, a child could break down all the elements that need to be completed (choose a topic, go to the library and check out books on this topic, make a list of supplies, purchase these supplies, and so on) and place these in a line as a plan of action.

Work together as a family, helping each other make flight plans for one or two goals each. Then ask:

- **What kind of flight plan could our family make to help us, as Paul wanted, to become more like Christ?**

The ideas your family comes up with will vary depending upon the ages and interests of your children. They might include a plan to have less fighting around the house, a plan to memorize Scripture, a plan for doing a family service project, and so on. Encourage creativ-

Age Adjustments

FOR YOUNGER CHILDREN, play a board game, such as Candyland or Chutes and Ladders, together. As you play, keep moving your marker out of turn, moving the wrong marker, going the wrong number of spaces, and so on. When your children are ready to give up from frustration with you, briefly discuss the plan of the game and how no one can win if this plan is not followed. Then think of things that cause your children to not "follow the plan" in their daily lives. This might include getting sidetracked and playing with toys instead of cleaning up the bedroom, getting into bed on time but not brushing teeth, or not feeding the dog. These are small tasks, but if we don't follow the correct plan, the job never gets finished or the goal is never reached.

FOR OLDER CHILDREN, pull out a large street map and have them plan a course from your home to a selected spot on the map. What roads will they take? Where will they stop for gas, food, or rest? How long will the trip take? How much will it cost?

As kids consider these factors, discuss how having a plan helps even a big task be completed. Knowing what might get in your way, knowing how to get around obstacles and so on will help when troubles arise. How is this like troubles or big jobs we face day to day? What obstacles might come up in your goal to be a virgin until you're married? What obstacles might keep you from growing closer to God? Think of a variety of realistic daily obstacles and plans to avoid or get around these.

ity while being realistic about what goals your family can complete. (You probably can't feed the entire population of the downtown area of your city . . . but with a little planning, who knows?)

Share: God wants us to finish what we start. With commitment, hard work, and planning, we're more likely to finish strong!

Over the next weeks, check in with family members to see how they're doing on reaching their various goals. And be sure to choose one or two family goals and work toward those in the coming weeks as well.

WRAP-UP

Gather everyone in a circle and have family members take turns answering this question: **What's one thing you've learned about God today?**

Next, tell kids you've got a new "Life Slogan" you'd like to share with them.

Life Slogan: Today's Life Slogan is this: "Do your best all along, and you'll be sure to finish strong!" Have family members repeat the slogan two or three times to help them learn it. Then encourage them to practice saying it during the week so they can talk about it at your next family night session.

Close in Prayer: Allow time for each family member to share prayer concerns and answers to prayer. Then close your time together with prayer for each concern. Thank God for making families, especially your family! Take time to thank God for each family member, mentioning one special quality you're thankful for about that person.

Remember to record prayer requests here so you can refer to them in the future as you see God answering them.

Additional Resources:

Adam Raccoon and the Race to Victory Mountain by Glen Keane (ages 4–7)
Bible Greats Noah Playset (ages 1–3)
Bartholomew Beaver and the Stupendous Splash by Michael Waite (ages 4–7)
Baby Bible Noah's Soft Ark Playset (ages 5–10)
Home Run Rudy and the Great Escape by Janet Garman (ages 8–12)

11: Standing Strong

Exploring how to take a stand for our belief in God

Scripture
- 2 Timothy 3:1-5—Godlessness of the world.
- 2 Timothy 3:12-17—Guidance can be found in God's Word.
- Matthew 12:30—We are either for Christ or against Christ.

ACTIVITY OVERVIEW		
Activity	Summary	Pre-Session Prep
Activity 1: The Heat Is On!	Contrast common culture to God's Word.	You'll need a current newspaper and a Bible.
Activity 2: Right versus Popular	Explore the effect of peer pressure.	You'll need a piece of paper, a pencil, and a ruler.
Activity 3: Mixed Up?	Compare God and sin to oil and water.	You'll need a glass, water, cooking oil, a spoon, and a Bible.

Main Points:
— We must know God's Word to know what kind of stand to take.

— Even when we are not in the majority, we may be in the right.

— We must either choose to stand for Christ or reject Christ.

LIFE SLOGAN: "When put on demand, just make a stand."

Make it your own
In the space provided below, outline the flow and add any additional ideas to guide you through the process of conducting this family night.

Prayer & Praise Items
In the space provided below, list any items you wish to pray about or give praise for during this family night session.

Journal
In the space provided below, capture a record of any fun or meaningful things which happened during this family night session.

Session Tip

We intentionally have provided more material than we would expect to be used in a single "Family Night" session. You know your family's unique interests and life circumstances best, so feel free to adapt this lesson to meet your family members' needs. Remember, short and simple is better than long and comprehensive.

WARM-UP

Open with Prayer: Begin by having a family member pray, asking God to help everyone in the family understand more about Him through this time. After prayer, review your last lesson by asking these questions:

- **What do you remember from our last lesson?**
- **Do you remember the Life Slogan?**
- **What was one fun thing we did during our last lesson?**
- **How has what we learned last week changed your actions in the past few days?**

Share: During our time today we'll be learning how to take a stand for what we believe.

ACTIVITY 1: The Heat Is On!

Point: We must know God's Word to know what kind of stand to take.

Supplies: You'll need a current newspaper and a Bible.

Activity: Look through the pages of the newspaper together and pick out articles on acts of evil, cruelty, or unrighteousness. Obviously, articles on war, rape, murder, and beatings are included, but look further for articles where someone was greedy, lied about another, refused to forgive, and so on. Read these articles, or at least summarize them together.

After you've read several articles, turn to the section of your paper where movies are listed and reviewed. As you read through the listings of the movies, have family members tell what they know

Age Adjustments

This activity may be upsetting for MANY YOUNG CHILDREN. They aren't ready to be exposed to the cruelties of the world. Instead, play a game with them.

Create a simple maze in your living room. Have one family member prepare to go through the maze while another family member stands on a chair at the end of the maze. The goal of the child going through the maze is to maintain eye contact with the person on the chair during the whole trek through the maze. The person on the chair can give directions if needed. Other family members should hover about and try to distract the child going through the maze. Don't allow any touching, but the distracters can tell jokes; call out things like, "Look out!" or "Look behind you!" or wave things in front of the person going through the maze.

Let each person take a turn, seeing how well each person does at not being distracted.

Then talk with your children about how others around us can try to get us to do the wrong thing. They try to distract us from doing what's right. Give simple examples, such as a neighbor child who encourages your child to spread jam on the wallpaper and then lie about who did it, or someone who is mean to others and gets everyone feeling crabby instead of loving. Make the point that God wants us to focus on what is right to do, and to tell others no when they try to get us to do wrong things.

CHALLENGE OLDER CHILDREN AND TEENAGERS to consider how they can be witnesses for God and lead others to Christ if they're always avoiding godless people. What's the meaning of being "in the world but not of the world"? Remind family members (including yourself) that filling our minds with things of the world won't make us stronger in our stand for God. Yet caring about those who don't know God does mean we'll have to befriend godless people. We have to determine what activities are going to strengthen our stand for God and help us shine God's light for others, and what activities are going to weaken our stand and take us away from God's light.

Help your older children and teenagers make practical decisions about friends, movies, music, and so on by encouraging them to consider whether what they're doing will strengthen their stand or weaken it. You might find yourself challenged as well!

or what they've heard about different movies. What movies are presenting nudity? violence? sex? bad language? greed? disobedience to authority?

Discuss these:

- **What comparisons can you make between the news** (what's real) and the movies we watch (what's fiction)?

- **How do you think what we watch in the movies becomes a part of our everyday lives?**
- **What about the music we listen to? the television shows we watch? the friends we choose? How do these shape our thoughts and actions?**

Share: In the Bible we can read about the last days, or that time before Christ returns.

 Read 2 Timothy 3:1-5, then discuss:
- **What common areas do you find between the description of godless people in the Bible and the news stories and movie reviews we've just read together?**
- **What is God telling us in this passage?** (We should have nothing to do with people who are like this.)
- **Why should we remove ourselves from this kind of company?** (Because they might rub off on us; because these people are living in sin and we should be living for God and trying to become more holy.)
- **Where do you most feel the influences or pressures of godless people?**
- **How do you try to take a stand for what God wants you to do? Is this hard or easy for you? Explain.**

Share: The godless people we read about in the Bible are all around us. And we're also affected by all the godlessness we allow into our minds and hearts. This puts a lot of pressure on us. We can choose to give in to the pressures and be like the godless people, or we can take a stand for what's right and follow God instead.

ACTIVITY 2: Right versus Popular

Point: Even when we are not in the majority, we may be in the right.

Supplies: You'll need a piece of paper, a pencil, and a ruler.

Activity: Ask the child who is most vulnerable to peer pressure to go into another room until you call him or her back. Draw three lines of nearly equal length on a sheet of paper and label them a, b, and c. Agree with the others in the room to insist that the second longest line is the longest line—no matter what the returning child says.

Bring the other child back into the room and ask him or her to identify which line is the longest. If he selects c (assuming c is actually the longest), look puzzled and respond by restating the assignment. "No, I said select the longest." Have the others in the room insist that the other line is longer. If this is done right, the child will likely give in and go along with the rest of you, selecting the second longest line.

Now, take out the ruler and show that c was actually the longest. Make the point that the child may not have been in the majority, but he or she was in the right.

 Read more of what Paul says about taking a stand in 2 Timothy 3:12-17.

Share: The Bible tells us it won't be easy being a Christian. People will laugh at us, put pressure on us to sin, and even punish us for our beliefs. But we learn here that we should be focusing on God, not on the world. We should be reading the Bible and testing what we see around us by God's Word. The Bible teaches us, corrects our thinking, trains us to be godly, and shows us where we're going in the wrong direction. We must know God's Word to know what kind of stand to take in the world today.

ACTIVITY 3: Mixed Up?

Point: We must either choose to stand for Christ or reject Christ.

Supplies: You'll need a clear glass jar, cooking oil, water, a spoon, and a Bible.

Activity: Have one of your children pour water into the clear glass, filling it halfway. Then have a child pour several inches of cooking oil into the same glass. Observe what happens. (If you like, mix a small amount of food coloring into the water to make the distinction between water and oil more clear.)

After the oil has settled on top of the water, give family members the opportunity to mix the combination with a spoon. Again, what happens?

Share: Oil and water don't mix. Even though the oil can be stirred

around in the water, it never truly mixes with the water. And as soon as the mixing stops, the oil immediately comes to the top of the water. Just like oil and water don't mix, good and bad don't mix. However, people around us try to mix good and bad together. Can you think of any examples of people mixing good with bad?

Examples might include:

*Television—it can bring both good shows and bad shows into our home.

*Music—it can have a good sound but a bad message.

*A person in authority might tell you to do the wrong thing.

*We might tell a lie to not hurt someone's feelings.

Encourage your family members to think of examples they have encountered in their own lives. Any mixture of the right thing for the wrong reason, or the wrong thing for the right reason, indicates someone trying to mix good and bad.

Then ask these questions:

• **When someone tries to mix good and bad, what do you think is the result?**

• **When is it hard for you to tell if something is good or bad? What do you do about this?**

Share: We have to make choices each day about mixing good and bad. We have to decide what to watch, read, and listen to, and who to hang around with. As we've already learned, the Bible is the best guide for helping us make these choices and stand up for what is right. As Christians, we are to be different than the world around us. I want to read you something else the Bible says about this topic.

Read Matthew 12:30 aloud, then discuss:

• **What does Jesus mean here?** (We are either with God or against God; if we're not doing God's will, we're doing Satan's will.)

• **Why do you think it's important that we determine whether we're with God or not?** (So we can know what to stand up for; so we can know how to make decisions; so we can choose what is right.)

Share: When we take a stand against what's wrong and for what's right, we might feel all alone. But God is with us. Our goal isn't to make our friends feel better about telling a lie, to laugh at sin, or to be sinners ourselves. Our goal is to bring glory to God and to become more like Christ. Remembering our goal helps us to make our stand even stronger. Just as oil and water are separate, God and sin are separate. We have to choose which one we'll stand for.

WRAP-UP

Gather everyone in a circle and have family members take turns answering this question: **What's one thing you've learned about God today?**

Next, tell kids you've got a new "Life Slogan" you'd like to share with them.

Life Slogan: Today's Life Slogan is this: "When put on demand, just take a stand." Have family members repeat the slogan two or three times to help them learn it. Then encourage them to practice saying it during the week so they can talk about it at your next family night session.

Close in Prayer: Allow time for each family member to share prayer concerns and answers to prayer. Then close your time together with prayer for each concern. Thank God for making families, especially your family! Take time to thank God for each family member, mentioning one special quality you're thankful for about that person.

Remember to record prayer requests here so you can refer to them in the future as you see God answering them.

Additional Resources:

Adam Raccoon and the Mighty Giant by Glen Keane (ages 4–7)
Face-to-Face with Women of the Bible by Nancy Simpson (ages 6–10)
In God We Trust by Timothy Crater and Ranelda Hunsicker (ages 8–12)
The New Kids Choices Game (ages 6–12)
The New Teen Choices Game (ages 12–18)

ⓔ 12: Control Yourself

Exploring the importance of self-control and discipline

Scripture
• 1 Peter 5:8-9—The devil is our enemy.
• 1 Peter 2:11-12—Abstain from sin.
• Proverbs 4:23—Guard your heart.

ACTIVITY OVERVIEW

Activity	Summary	Pre-Session Prep
Activity 1: Enemy Territory	Resist physical urges as a way of understanding self-control.	You'll need blindfolds, a timer, a feather, and a Bible.
Activity 2: Raise Your Hand	Train arms to raise and compare this to spiritual training.	You'll need a doorway in your home and a Bible.

Main Points:
—Self-control helps us resist the enemy.
—Discipline and training make us stronger.

LIFE SLOGAN: "Before the enemy takes his toll, get ahead with self-control."

Make it your own
In the space provided below, outline the flow and add any additional ideas to guide you through the process of conducting this family night.

Prayer & Praise Items
In the space provided below, list any items you wish to pray about or give praise for during this family night session.

Journal
In the space provided below, capture a record of any fun or meaningful things which happened during this family night session.

Session Tip

We intentionally have provided more material than we would expect to be used in a single "Family Night" session. You know your family's unique interests and life circumstances best, so feel free to adapt this lesson to meet your family members' needs. Remember, short and simple is better than long and comprehensive.

WARM-UP

Open with Prayer: Begin by having a family member pray, asking God to help everyone in the family understand more about Him through this time. After prayer, review your last lesson by asking these questions:

- **What do you remember from our last lesson?**
- **Do you remember the Life Slogan?**
- **What was one fun thing we did during our last lesson?**
- **How has what we learned last week changed your actions in the past few days?**

Share: Today's lesson will help us learn the importance of self-control.

ACTIVITY 1: Enemy Territory

Point: Self-control helps us resist the enemy.

Supplies: You'll need blindfolds, a watch or timer, a feather or other soft and "tickly" item, and a Bible.

Activity: Have all your children sit on the floor with no one touching another. Blindfold each child, then have everyone sit quietly while listening to you.

Share: I want each of you to pretend that you're in enemy territory. You're hidden under a small bush and there are enemy soldiers all around. The slightest move from you will alert them to your presence. You've got to hold perfectly still for three minutes. No twitching, talking, giggling, scratching, or anything! Go!

Begin the timer and watch to see how well your children can control themselves. After about a minute, take the feather and begin gently tickling your children with it. See if they flinch or if they're able to remain as still as stone.

After the three minutes are up, allow your children to blindfold you and any other adults in the family. Repeat the exercise, seeing how well you handle the pressures of holding still while all your children are bouncing about, feathers in hand!

When everyone has had a turn, remove all blindfolds and put away the feathers. Then discuss:

- **Was it hard or easy for you to keep perfectly still? Explain.**
- **If a real enemy was around and the situation I described was truly happening, do you think it would be easier or harder to hold still? Explain.**

Share: Believe it or not, there really is an enemy lurking around here. The Bible tells us about this enemy.

 Read 1 Peter 5:8-9 aloud, then discuss:

- **Who's the enemy the Bible tells us about?** (The devil.)
- **What's this enemy doing?** (Prowling like a roaring lion; looking for someone to devour.)
- **What do you think this means?** (The devil is always looking for ways to trick us; the devil is trying to defeat us; the devil is always looking for an opportunity to attack.)
- **What ways do you think the devil tries to "devour" or trick you?** (Answers will vary, but encourage family members to consider temptations and pressures they encounter. This might include temptations or pressures to cheat, to watch inappropriate movies or shows, to tell a lie, or to do any other wrong action.)
- **Why do you think it's important to have self-control?** (To be prepared to withstand enemy attacks; so we don't give in to temptations or pressures.)

 Read 1 Peter 2:11-12 aloud.

Share: We really are in a war against the devil and our sinful desires. This means we have to control our thoughts and actions. Then we'll be able to bring glory to God, and we'll remain strong in our faith. Self-control helps us resist the enemy.

Age Adjustments

CHILDREN OF ALL AGES may enjoy repeating the feather-tickling exercise, seeing if practice helps them train themselves not to move. This can help us understand that training and discipline give us more self-control.

ACTIVITY 2: Raise Your Hand

Point: Discipline and training make us stronger.

Supplies: You'll need a narrow doorway and a Bible.

Activity: Have one child stand in an open doorway. The doorway should be narrow enough for the child to easily touch both sides of the door frame at once.

Have the child raise his arms from his sides so that the outer part of the wrist is pressing against the door frame.

Explain that the child will need to press outward, toward the door frame, for 45 seconds. After this time is up, have the child move out of the doorway into the open room. Ask the child to raise his or her arms. They should rise effortlessly.

Repeat with other family members as often as children want.

Note: If none of your doorways are narrow enough, a child can do one arm instead of two, bracing against a parent or larger person if necessary.

Share: It was hard work pressing against the door, but this hard work made raising your arms easy. How do you think this is like training ourselves to be strong in self-control? (It's hard to train our minds, but it makes it easier to resist the devil and sin later.)

Share: When we train ourselves to say no to sin and things that are not honoring to God, we win the battle over the devil.

Read Proverbs 4:23 and ask:
- **How do we guard our hearts?** (Protect ourselves from sin; say no to wrong things; keep away from temptations and pressures.)

Share: Just like we can train our arms to rise easily, we can train our minds to avoid the devil and sin. We have to work at this; it isn't easy. But the reward is worth the work!

WRAP-UP

Gather everyone in a circle and have family members take turns answering this question: **What's one thing you've learned about God today?**

Next, tell kids you've got a new "Life Slogan" you'd like to share with them.

Life Slogan: Today's Life Slogan is this: "Before the enemy takes his toll, get ahead with self-control." Have family members repeat the slogan two or three times to help them learn it. Then encourage them to practice saying it during the week so they can talk about it at your next family night session.

Close in Prayer: Allow time for each family member to share prayer concerns and answers to prayer. Then close your time together with prayer for each concern. Thank God for making families, especially your family! Take time to thank God for each family member, mentioning one special quality you're thankful for about that person.

Remember to record prayer requests here so you can refer to them in the future as you see God answering them.

Additional Resources:

Hip Hop and His Famous Face by Gary Oliver and Norman Wright (ages 4–7)
The Ten Commandments for Children by Lois Rock (ages 4–7)
Time Out! by Janet Holm McHenry (ages 7–10)

Age Adjustments

CHILDREN OF ALL AGES will learn more about this topic by visiting an animal training school. Make arrangements to view a session, and observe together how owners and their pets work so the animal will be obedient. Then make comparisons between our spiritual lives and the animal training. How can a dog resist the urge to bark at a doorbell? How can an animal resist the urge to eat food placed directly in front of it? In the same way, how can we resist temptations the devil places before us?

Another field trip for children of all ages is to a fire station. Again, call ahead to ask for a tour, then observe the training these men and women must endure. Why do they work so hard? What is the purpose of their training? What is the reward of their training? How is this training like the training we must do with our minds?

How to Lead Your Child to Christ

SOME THINGS TO CONSIDER AHEAD OF TIME:

1. Realize that God is more concerned about your child's eternal destiny and happiness than you are. "The Lord is not slow in keeping his promise.... He is patient with you, not wanting anyone to perish, but everyone to come to repentance" (2 Peter 3:9).

2. Pray specifically beforehand that God will give you insights and wisdom in dealing with each child on his or her maturity level.

3. Don't use terms like "take Jesus into your heart," "dying and going to hell," and "accepting Christ as your personal Savior." Children are either too literal ("How does Jesus breathe in my heart?") or the words are too clichéd and trite for their understanding.

4. Deal with each child alone, and don't be in a hurry. Make sure he or she understands. Discuss. Take your time.

A FEW CAUTIONS:

1. When drawing children to Himself, Jesus said for others to "allow" them to come to Him (see Mark 10:14). Only with adults did He use the term "compel" (see Luke 14:23). Do not compel children.

2. Remember that unless the Holy Spirit is speaking to the child, there will be no genuine heart experience of regeneration. Parents, don't get caught up in the idea that Jesus will return the day before you were going to speak to your child about salvation and that it will be too late. Look at God's character—He *is* love! He is not dangling your child's soul over hell. Wait on God's timing.

   Pray with faith, believing. Be concerned, but don't push.

THE PLAN:

1. **God loves you.** Recite John 3:16 with your child's name in place of "the world."

2. **Show the child his or her need of a Savior.**

   a. Deal with sin carefully. There is one thing that cannot enter heaven—sin.

   b. Be sure your child knows what sin is. Ask him to name some (things common to children—lying, sassing, disobeying, etc.). Sin is doing or thinking anything wrong according to God's Word. It is breaking God's Law.

   c. Ask the question "Have you sinned?" If the answer is no, do not continue. Urge him to come and talk to you again when he does feel that he has sinned. Dismiss him. You may want to have prayer first, however, thanking God "for this young child who is willing to do what is right." Make it easy for him to talk to you again, but do not continue. Do not say, "Oh, yes, you have too sinned!" and then name some. With children, wait for God's conviction.

   d. If the answer is yes, continue. He may even give a personal illustration of some sin he has done recently or one that has bothered him.

   e. Tell him what God says about sin: We've all sinned ("There is no one righteous, not even one," Rom. 3:10). And because of that sin, we can't get to God ("For the wages of sin is death . . ." Rom. 6:23). So He had to come to us (". . . but the gift of God is eternal life in Christ Jesus our Lord," Rom. 6:23).

   f. Relate God's gift of salvation to Christmas gifts—we don't earn them or pay for them; we just accept them and are thankful for them.

3. **Bring the child to a definite decision.**

   a. Christ must be received if salvation is to be possessed.

   b. Remember, do not force a decision.

   c. Ask the child to pray out loud in her own words. Give her some things she could say if she seems unsure. Now be prepared for a blessing! (It is best to avoid having the child repeat a memorized prayer after you. Let her think, and make it personal.)*

d. After salvation has occurred, pray for her out loud. This is a good way to pronounce a blessing on her.

4. **Lead your child into assurance.**

Show him that he will have to keep his relationship open with God through repentance and forgiveness (just like with his family or friends), but that God will always love him ("Never will I leave you; never will I forsake you," Heb. 13:5).

* If you wish to guide your child through the prayer, here is some suggested language.

"Dear God, I know that I am a sinner [have child name specific sins he or she acknowledged earlier, such as lying, stealing, disobeying, etc.]. I know that Jesus died on the cross to pay for all my sins. I ask you to forgive me of my sins. I believe that Jesus died for me and rose from the dead, and I accept Him as my Savior. Thank You for loving me. In Jesus' name. Amen."

Cumulative Topical Index

TOPIC	SCRIPTURE	WHAT YOU'LL NEED	WHERE TO FIND IT
The Acts of the Sinful Nature and the Fruit of the Spirit	Gal. 5:19-26	3x5 cards or paper, markers, and tape	Book 1, p. 43
All Have Sinned	Rom. 3:23	Raw eggs, bucket of water	Book 2, p. 89
Avoid Things that Keep Us from Growing	Eph. 4:14-15; Heb. 5:11-14	Seeds, plants at various stages of growth or a garden or nursery to tour, Bible	Book 3, p. 77
Bad Company Corrupts Good Character	1 Cor. 15:33	Small ball, string, slips of paper, pencil, yarn or masking tape, Bible	Book 1, p. 103
Be Thankful for Good Friends		Art supplies, markers	Book 1, p. 98
Being Content with What We Have	Phil. 4:11-13	Bible, candle	Book 3, p. 17
Christ Is Who We Serve	Col. 3:23-24	Paper, scissors, pens	Book 1, p. 50
Christians Should Be Joyful Each Day	Lam. 3:22-23; Ps. 118:24	Small plastic bottle, cork to fit bottle opening, water, vinegar, baking soda, paper towel, Bible	Book 3, p. 67
Commitment and Hard Work Are Needed to Finish Strong	Gen. 6:5-22	Jigsaw puzzle, Bible	Book 3, p. 83
The Consequence of Sin Is Death	Ps. 19:1-6	Dominoes	Book 2, p. 57
Creation	Gen. 1:1; Ps. 19:1-6; Rom. 1:20	Nature book or video, Bible	Book 1, p. 17
David and Bathsheba	2 Sam. 11:1–12:14	Bible	Book 2, p. 90
Description of Heaven	Rev. 21:3-4, 10-27	Bible, drawing supplies	Book 2, p. 76
Difficulty Can Help Us Grow	Jer. 32:17; Luke 18:27	Bible, card game like Old Maid or Crazy Eight	Book 3, p. 33

TOPIC	SCRIPTURE	WHAT YOU'LL NEED	WHERE TO FIND IT
Discipline and Training Make Us Stronger	Prov. 4:23	Narrow doorway, Bible	Book 3, p. 103
Don't Be Yoked with Unbelievers	2 Cor. 16:17–17:1	Milk, food coloring	Book 1, p. 105
Don't Give Respect Based on Material Wealth	Eph. 6:1-8; 1 Peter 2:13-17; Ps. 119:17; James 2:1-2; 1 Tim. 4:12	Large sheet of paper, tape, a pen, Bible	Book 1, p. 64
Even If We're Not in the Majority, We May Be Right	2 Tim. 3:12-17	Piece of paper, pencil, ruler	Book 3, p. 95
Every Day Is a Gift from God	Prov. 16:9	Bible	Book 3, p. 69
Evil Hearts Say Evil Words	Prov. 15:2-8; Luke 6:45; Eph. 4:29	Bible, small mirror	Book 1, p. 79
The Fruit of the Spirit	Gal. 5:22-23; Luke 3:8; Acts 26:20	Blindfold and Bible	Book 2, p. 92
God Allows Testing to Help Us Mature	James 1:2-4	Bible	Book 2, p. 44
God Can Do the Impossible	John 6:1-14	Bible, sturdy plank (6 or more inches wide and 6 to 8 feet long), a brick or similar object, snack of fish and crackers	Book 3, p. 31
God Created Us	Isa. 45:9, 64:8; Ps. 139:13	Bible and video of potter with clay	Book 2, p. 43
God Doesn't Want Us to Worry	Matt. 6:25-34; Phil. 4:6-7; Ps. 55:22	Bible, paper, pencils	Book 3, p. 39
God Forgives Those Who Confess Their Sins	1 John 1:9	Sheets of paper, tape, Bible	Book 2, p. 58
God Gave Jesus a Message for Us	John 1:14, 18; 8:19; 12:49-50	Goldfish in water or bug in jar, water	Book 2, p. 66
God Gives and God Can Take Away	Luke 12:13-21	Bible, timer with bell or buzzer, large bowl of small candies, smaller bowl for each child	Book 3, p. 15
God Is Holy	Ex. 3:1-6	Masking tape, baby powder or corn starch, broom, Bible	Book 1, p. 31
God Is Invisible, Powerful, and Real	John 1:18, 4:24; Luke 24:36-39	Balloons, balls, refrigerator magnets, Bible	Book 1, p. 15
God Knew His Plans for Us	Jer. 29:11	Two puzzles and a Bible	Book 2, p. 19
God Knows All About Us	Ps. 139:2-4; Matt. 10:30	3x5 cards, a pen	Book 2, p. 17

TOPIC	SCRIPTURE	WHAT YOU'LL NEED	WHERE TO FIND IT
God Knows Everything	Isa. 40:13-14; Eph. 4:1-6	Bible	Book 1, p. 15
God Loves Us So Much, He Sent Jesus	John 3:16; Eph. 2:8-9	I.O.U. for each family member	Book 1, p. 34
God Made Our Family Unique by Placing Each of Us in It	Prov. 27:17	Different color paint for each family member, toothpicks or paintbrushes to dip into paint, white paper, Bible	Book 2, p. 110
God Made Us in His Image	Gen. 1:24-27	Play dough or clay and Bible	Book 2, p. 24
God Provides a Way Out of Temptation	1 Cor. 10:12-13; James 1:13-14; 4:7; 1 John 2:15-17	Bible	Book 1, p. 88
God Wants Us to Be Diligent in Our Work	Prov. 6:6-11; 1 Thes. 4:11-12	Video about ants or picture book or encyclopedia; Bible	Book 3, p. 55
God Wants Us to Get Closer to Him	James 4:8; 1 John 4:7-12	Hidden Bibles, clues to find them	Book 2, p. 33
God Wants Us to Work and Be Helpful	2 Thes. 3:6-15	Several undone chores, Bible	Book 3, p. 53
God Will Send the Holy Spirit	John 14:23-26; 1 Cor. 2:12	Flashlights, small treats, Bible	Book 1, p. 39
God's Covenant with Noah	Gen. 8:13-21; 9:8-17	Bible, paper, crayons or markers	Book 2, p. 52
Guarding the Gate to Our Minds	Prov. 4:13; 2 Cor. 11:3; Phil. 4:8	Bible, poster board for each family member, old magazines, glue, scissors, markers	Book 3, p. 23
The Holy Spirit Helps Us	Eph. 1:17; John 14:15-17; Acts 1:1-11; Eph. 3:16-17; Rom. 8:26-27; 1 Cor. 2:11-16	Bible	Book 2, p. 99
Honor the Holy Spirit, Don't Block Him	1 John 4:4; 1 Cor. 6:19-20	Bible, blow dryer or vacuum cleaner with exit hose, a Ping-Pong ball	Book 3, p. 47
Honor Your Parents	Ex. 20:12	Paper, pencil, treats, umbrella, soft objects, masking tape, pen, Bible	Book 1, p. 55
The Importance of Your Name Being Written in the Book of Life	Rev. 20:11-15; 21:27	Bible, phone book, access to other books with family name	Book 2, p. 74

TOPIC	SCRIPTURE	WHAT YOU'LL NEED	WHERE TO FIND IT
It's Important to Listen to Jesus' Message			Book 2, p. 68
Jesus Dies on the Cross	John 14:6	6-foot 2x4, 3-foot 2x4, hammers, nails, Bible	Book 1, p. 33
Jesus Took the Punishment We Deserve	Rom. 6:23; John 3:16; Rom. 5:8-9	Bathrobe, list of bad deeds	Book 1, p. 26
Jesus Washes His Followers' Feet	John 13:1-17	Bucket of warm, soapy water, towels, Bible	Book 1, p. 63
Joshua and the Battle of Jericho	Josh. 1:16-18; 6:1-21	Paper, pencil, dots on paper that when connected form a star	Book 1, p. 57
Knowing God's Word Helps Us Know What Stand to Take	2 Tim. 3:1-5	Current newspaper, Bible	Book 3, p. 93
The More We Know God, the More We Know His Voice	John 10:1-6	Bible	Book 2, p. 35
Nicodemus Asks Jesus About Being Born Again	John 3:7, 50-51; 19:39-40	Bible, paper, pencil, costume	Book 2, p. 81
Obedience Has Good Rewards		Planned outing everyone will enjoy, directions on 3x5 cards, number cards	Book 1, p. 59
Our Minds Should Be Filled with Good, Not Evil	Phil 4:8; Ps. 119:9, 11	Bible, bucket of water, several large rocks	Book 3, p. 26
Parable of the Talents	Matt. 25:14-30	Bible	Book 1, p. 73
Parable of the Vine and Branches	John 15:1-8	Tree branch, paper, pencils, Bible	Book 1, p. 95
Planning Helps Us Finish Strong	Phil. 3:10-14	Flight map on p. 86, paper, pencils, Bible	Book 3, p. 85
The Responsibiities of Families	Eph. 5:22-33; 6:1-4	Photo albums, Bible	Book 2, p. 101
Self-control Helps Us Resist the Enemy	1 Peter 5:8-9; 1 Peter 2:11-12	Blindfold, watch or timer, feather or other "tickly" item, Bible	Book 3, p. 101
Serve One Another in Love	Gal. 5:13	Bag of small candies, at least three per child	Book 1, p. 47

TOPIC	SCRIPTURE	WHAT YOU'LL NEED	WHERE TO FIND IT
Sin and Busyness Interfere with Our Prayers	Luke 10:38-42; Ps. 46:10; Matt. 5:23-24; 1 Peter 3:7	Bible, two paper cups, two paper clips, long length of fishing line or paper, megaphones, and socks	Book 3, p. 61
Sin Separates Humanity	Gen. 3:1-24	Bible, clay creations, piece of hardened clay or play dough	Book 2, p. 25
Some Places Aren't Open to Everyone		Book or magazine with "knock-knock" jokes	Book 2, p. 73
Some Things in Life Are Out of Our Control		Blindfolds	Book 2, p. 41
Temptation Takes Our Eyes Off God		Fishing pole, items to catch, timer, Bible	Book 1, p. 85
Those Who Don't Believe Are Foolish	Ps. 44:1	Ten small pieces of paper, pencil, Bible	Book 1, p. 19
The Tongue Is Small but Powerful	James 3:3-12	Video, news magazine, or picture book showing devastation of fire, match, candle, Bible	Book 1, p. 77
We All Sin	Rom. 3:23	Target and items to throw	Book 1, p. 23
We Can Communicate with Each Other			Book 2, p. 65
We Can Help Each Other	Prov. 27:17	Masking tape, bowl of unwrapped candies, rulers, yardsticks, or dowel rods	Book 2, p. 110
We Can Love by Helping Those in Need	Heb. 13:1-3		Book 1, p. 48
We Can Show Love through Respecting Family Members		Paper and pen	Book 1, p. 66
We Can't Take Back the Damage of Our Words		Tube of toothpaste for each child, $10 bill	Book 1, p. 78
We Deserve Punishment for Our Sins	Rom. 6:23	Dessert, other materials as decided	Book 1, p. 24
We Have a New Life in Christ	John 3:3; 2 Cor. 5:17	Video or picture book of caterpillar forming a cocoon then a butterfly, or a tadpole becoming a frog, or a seed becoming a plant	Book 2, p. 93

TOPIC	SCRIPTURE	WHAT YOU'LL NEED	WHERE TO FIND IT
We Know Others by Our Relationships with Them		Copies of questionnaire, pencils, Bible	Book 2, p. 31
We Must Be in Constant Contact with God		Blindfolds	Book 3, p. 63
We Must Choose to Obey	Matt. 12:30	3x5 cards or slips of paper, markers, and tape	Book 1, p. 43
We Must Either Choose Christ or Reject Christ		Clear glass jar, cooking oil, water, spoon, Bible	Book 3, p. 96
We Must Learn How Much Responsibility We Can Handle	1 Peter 2:2	Building blocks, watch with second hand, paper, pencil	Book 1, p. 71
We Need to Grow Physically, Emotionally, and Spiritually		Photograph albums or videos of your children at different ages, tape measure, bathroom scale, Bible	Book 3, p. 75
We Reap What We Sow	Gal. 6:7	Candy bar, Bible	Book 1, p. 55
We Shouldn't Value Possessions Over Everything Else	1 Tim. 6:7-8	Box is optional	Book 3, p. 18
With Help, Life Is a Lot Easier		Supplies to do the chore you choose	Book 2, p. 101
Wolves in Sheeps' Clothing	Matt. 7:15-20	Ten paper sacks, a marker, ten small items, Bible	Book 1, p. 97
Worrying Doesn't Change Anything		Board, inexpensive doorbell buzzer, a 9-volt battery, extra length of electrical wire, a large bolt, assorted tools	Book 3, p. 37
You Look Like the Person in Whose Image You Are Created		Paper roll, crayons, markers, pictures of your kids and of yourself as a child	Book 2, p. 23

Welcome to the Family!

Heritage
Builders
Helping You Build a Family of Faith

We hope you've enjoyed this book. Heritage Builders was founded in 1995 by
three fathers with a passion for the next generation. As a new ministry of Focus
on the Family, Heritage Builders strives to equip, train and motivate
parents to become intentional about building a strong spiritual heritage.

It's quite a challenge for busy parents to find ways to build a spiritual foundation for their families—especially in a way they enjoy and understand. Through
activities and participation, children can learn biblical truth in
a way they can understand, enjoy—and *remember.*

Passing along a heritage of Christian faith to your family is a parent's highest
calling. Heritage Builders' goal is to encourage and empower you in this great
mission with practical resources and inspiring ideas that really work—
and help your children develop a lasting love for God.

***

How To Reach Us

For more information, visit our Heritage Builders Web site! Log on to
www.heritagebuilders.com to discover new resources, sample activities, and
ideas to help you pass on a spiritual heritage. To request any of these resources,
simply call Focus on the Family at 1-800-A-FAMILY
(1-800-232-6459) or in Canada, call 1-800-661-9800. Or send your request
to Focus on the Family, Colorado Springs, CO 80995.
In Canada, write Focus on the Family, P.O. Box 9800,
Stn. Terminal, Vancouver, B.C. V6B 4G3

To learn more about Focus on the Family or to find out if there is an
associate office in your country, please visit www. family.org

We'd love to hear from you!

Try These Heritage Builders Resources!

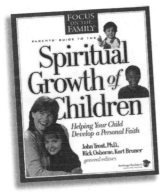

Parents' Guide to the
Spiritual Growth of Children

Building a foundation of faith in your children can be easy–
and fun!–with help from the *Parents' Guide to the Spiritual Growth
of Children*. Through simple and practical advice,
this comprehensive guide shows you how to build a
spiritual training plan for your family and it explains
what to teach your children at different ages.

Bedtime Blessings

Strengthen the precious bond between you, your child and God by making
Bedtime Blessings a special part of your evenings together. From best-selling author John
Trent, Ph.D., and Heritage Builders, this book is filled with stories, activities and blessing
prayers to help you practice the biblical model of "blessing."

My Time With God

Send your child on an amazing adventure—a self-guided tour through God's Word! *My Time
With God* shows your 8- to 12-year-old how to get to know God regularly in exciting ways.
Through 150 days' worth of fun facts and mind-boggling trivia, prayer starters, and
interesting questions, your child will discover how awesome God really is!

The Singing Bible

Children ages 2 to 7 will love *The Singing Bible*, which sets the Bible to music with over
50 fun, sing-along songs! Lead your child through Scripture by using *The Singing Bible*
to introduce the story of Jonah, the Ten Commandments and more.
This is a fun, fast-paced journey kids will remember.

• • •

Visit our Heritage Builders Web Site! Log on to
www.heritagebuilders. com to discover new resources,
sample activities, and ideas to help you pass on a spiritual heritage.
To request any of these resources, simply call Focus on the Family at
1-800-A-FAMILY (1-800-232-6459) or in Canada, call 1-800-661-9800.
Or send your request to Focus on the Family, Colorado Springs, CO
80995. In Canada, Write Focus on the Family, P.O. Box 9800,
Stn. Terminal, Vancouver, B.C. V6B 4G3.

Helping You Build a Family of Faith

Every family has a heritage—a spiritual, emotional, and social
legacy passed from one generation to the next. There are four
main areas we at Heritage Builders recommend parents consider
as they plan to pass their faith to their children:

Family Fragrance

Every family's home has a fragrance. Heritage Builders encourages parents to
create a home environment that fosters a sweet, Christ-centered AROMA
of love through Affection, Respect, Order, Merriment, and Affirmation.

Family Traditions

Whether you pass down stories, beliefs and/or customs, traditions can help
you establish a special identity for your family. Heritage Builders encourages
parents to set special "milestones" for their children to help guide them and
move them through their spiritual development.

Family Compass

Parents have the unique task of setting standards for normal,
healthy living through their attitudes, actions and beliefs. Heritage
Builders encourages parents to give their children the moral navigation
tools they need to succeed on the roads of life.

Family Moments

Creating special, teachable moments with their children is one of a parent's
most precious and sometimes, most difficult responsibilities. Heritage Builders
encourages parents to capture little moments throughout the day to teach
and impress values, beliefs, and biblical principles onto their children.

We look forward to standing alongside you as you seek to impart the Lord's
care and wisdom onto the next generation—onto your children.

Heritage
Builders

Helping You Build a Family of Faith